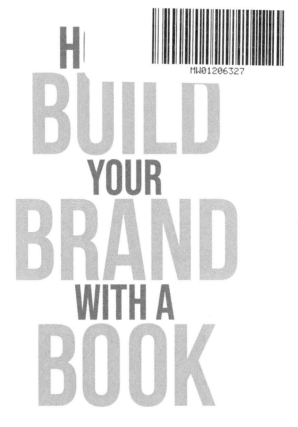

HOW TO BUILD YOUR BRAND WITH A BOOK

DISTINGUISHING YOURSELF AS A PUBLISHED EXPERT

SECOND EDITION

By Scott Turman and Zoe Rose

REVIEWS

"This was a fun and informative read. Self-publishing a book is a great way to take your idea and get it into the real world. There's never been a better time to be an author, and this book will give you all the essentials you'll need to make that happen."

~ Will Bussey
Marketing Director

"Stop wishing for instant brand awareness through viral sensationalism. Put in the work guided by *How to Build Your Brand with a Book*, and your published work will generate lasting brand value. This book is well organized, easy to follow, and packed with every essential element to create a published work to build lasting awareness of your branded expertise. With this book, you are equipped with the publishing expertise necessary to identify and overcome the obstacles to publishing a work which builds lasting awareness of your branded expertise."

~ Kevin Hagan
Contract Manager

"Are you launching a new product or service and need to explain its features and benefits to your target audience? Or, maybe you're trying to break into a competitive market and are seeking a unique way to tell your story and distinguish your brand. Then, you need to read *How to Build Your Brand with a Book*, which offers THE guide for first-time authors who want to build an online presence, create product awareness, and even capture media attention by writing a book to publicize their product and promote their business."

~ Shane Brey
Inventor, Small Business Owner, and Marketing Connoisseur

"A top-shelf resource for anyone who's ever wanted to write a book and get published. *How to Build Your Brand with a Book* is like having a best friend in the publishing business giving you guidance. It's chock-full of insider information and can help you learn what the professionals know."

~ Fred Grob
Senior Sales Engineer

"How to Build Your Brand with a Book is an extremely valuable roadmap to publishing your own book. It allows you to reflect on your own brand and then guides you on ways to articulate this to your readers by sharing your knowledge, successes, expertise, wisdom, and sought-after ideas you know that are highly worth sharing. Everyone is looking for answers. This is the entire start-to-finish publishing process. Truly a thumbs-up!**"**

~ Gina Jennings
Retired Higher Education Administrator

"Scott Turman and Zoe Rose provide a thorough and easy to follow framework for those considering writing a book. From start-to-finish, they progress through the publishing process with highly-informative discussions of current options. Definitely a timely and relevant resource that any aspiring author will value!**"**

~ Leonard Wise
Program Manager

"As someone who worked for a large library system, I have witnessed the struggles of those who are attempting to write a book. This publication covers every facet of writing and would be an extremely helpful resource for anyone wishing to write their own book.**"**

~ Carla S.
Retired Information Services Library Aide

"Right from the start, I was impressed with How to Build Your Brand with a Book, which encourages an author to set a foundation to build from. That foundation and the practical, achievable methods that follow provide a straightforward path to publication.**"**

~ Jon Denham
Director of Sales

"A must-read for anyone who is considering writing a book, building a brand, or just looking to lift the lid on Pandora's box for a peek into the publishing world. A quick read with actionable summaries after each category makes it easy to follow and manageable to obtain a finished product. Well done, what a wonderful guide.**"**

~ Stefanie Benotti
Development Consultant

"Writing and editing a book, and then having the manuscript formatted and cover designed, followed by somehow getting it published, always seemed so unattainable. Not anymore! How to Build Your Brand with a Book offers a step-by-step guide for first-time authors seeking to distinguish themselves as published industry experts. This really is a game-changer and will shake things up!**"**

~ Packy Lyden
Executive Director

"I was enlightened by the conciseness of *How to Build Your Brand with a Book*. The authors clearly lay out the map to writing successfully with clear and articulate steps. These comprehensive reasons are laid out in a common-sense style designed to propel success."

~ Geoff Carroll
Online Marketing Expert

"There's writer's block, and then there's writing-a-book block. Even if you generally don't struggle with the former, the latter endeavor of expanding your writing into a book can be quite daunting. From mapping out your topic into cohesive chapters to getting your book into the hands of your desired audience, this book aims to guide you through the steps along the path to becoming a published author."

~ Laurine Megna-Davis
Elementary Teacher, Mentor, and Reading Specialist

"Looking to distinguish yourself from other business owners? This book is a comprehensive guide that details how to write your own book to help your brand stick out from the crowd and position you as an industry leader."

~ Rocky Verteramo
Realtor and Entrepreneur

"Insightful, informative, and descriptive, *How to Build Your Brand with a Book* is a must-read for any aspiring authors looking to write and publish their own book. A detailed step-by-step guide, the reader is led through the entire literary process from writing and publishing a book to marketing and distribution."

~ Michael Clancy
Business Development Manager

"If you're thinking about writing a book or having a book published, then this book is for you. It is easy to read with specific step-by-step instructions in everything you need to know about writing, publishing, and marketing your book."

~ Kathryn Matrunola
Nonprofit Administrator

"A well-written and concise step-by-step process to guide you through publishing your own book. It discusses all modern aspects of the publishing world and the summaries at the end of each chapter are a great checklist to help ensure you have done everything necessary to be a success."

~ Rory Kolarich
Regional Sales Manager

"Writing is something we learn in elementary school, and some people are more naturally gifted than others. However, everyone has a story or a speciality. In *How to Build Your Brand with a Book*, the steps to writing a book are simply and thoroughly explained. It's so much more than taking a pen to a piece of paper, but it can be done! A must-read for anyone who has a story that warrants writing a book."

~ Karen Saum
Marketing Strategist

"Organized, pointed, and specific, *How to Build Your Brand with a Book* will guide you on your journey to publishing. By walking you through the process, this text is a must-have for anyone entering the literary world."

~ James T. Gendreau
Commercial Real Estate Developer

"*How to Build Your Brand with a Book* is direct, cuts out the fluff, and walks the reader through the steps necessary to go from just a thought or desire, to actually producing a manuscript, and ultimately producing a viable, publishable book! It addresses items that you probably have briefly thought about, or may have thought they were daunting (like producing a front and back cover, or acquiring an ISBN), to easily give directions on how to complete your book!"

~ John Haggerty
Integration Architect

"This book was an easy read and full of great insights for anyone who wants to have a real practical step by step roadmap to finally do what it takes to start that book! This book doesn't disappoint. You can read it chapter by chapter, or all the way through and then go back and use the step-by-step plan."

~ Delia Algeo
Senior Manager

"I'm a person who has considered getting my own book for a while, but where do you start? This is an ABSOLUTE must have resource on the topic, especially if you're planning on going about the book writing yourself."

~ Thomas Jepsen
Entrepreneur

"As a mentor once told me, your network is your net worth. Great book to prepare any entrepreneur to think of all interactions as a brand building exercise that generates value. Can't wait to get my first book launched!"

~ Craig Ceccanti
CEO & President

ISBN: 978-1-956464-04-7

Edited by Emily Batdorf and Ed Trifone.

BRIGHTRAY
PUBLISHING
BrightRayPublishing.com

TABLE OF CONTENTS

PART V: Publishing

PART VI: Launching Your Book

DEDICATION

To my beautiful wife.

I have been told by multiple people on multiple occasions in multiple countries that you must be an incredibly patient woman in order to deal with me. I love you bunches!

To Clint Christensen, thank you for being my friend and consigliere.

To Peter Kramer, who made the last years of my mother's life happy, comfortable, and full of love.

~ Scott

In memory of Steve Burton, the coolest man in Ohio. Your stories were better than anything I could ever write, especially the ones I wasn't supposed to hear.

In memory of Susan Hoover, the woman who proved that every kid is capable with enough encouragement. Thank you for believing in me.

~ Zoe

PREFACE

Why Write a Book?

If you've picked up this book, then there's an almost certain chance you're considering writing one yourself. If so, congratulations! This is an excellent first step toward that goal. This book is for people who want to write a book to tell their story and build their brand. If this sounds like you, keep reading. If you're not sure what this process entails, continue on.

Publishing a book is the single best way to build your brand. Furthermore, a book is the quickest and most effective way to distinguish yourself as a published expert in your industry, gain attention for you and/or your business, and reap the other benefits of being someone who has written a book in their field. (We'll delve into what exactly your book can accomplish and how to achieve the most from it later.)

Most everyone, especially prominent business executives and successful entrepreneurs, has probably thought of writing a book at some point. Like skydiving or visiting Europe, writing a book is a goal many people have on their bucket lists. If it was as easy as crossing it off, just about everybody would be a published author.

And that's exactly why not everyone is an author—in the same way we aren't all daredevils or world travelers—because writing a book is *hard*. It takes time, skill, drive, and a desire that most people just don't have. A book evolves from either a great idea or someone with a story worth sharing; usually, most of us don't have either.

In reality, the vast majority of us probably wouldn't even finish writing the first chapter. We don't mean to be critical. Scott knows firsthand how difficult it can be to convey experience into a published book—he spent almost ten years working through the process himself!

His first book centers on his unique knowledge as a small business CEO dealing with recruiters who specialize solely in the IT industry. A select few recruiters earn their living by taking advantage of highly skilled programmers who may not know how to negotiate equitable compensation for their services, and some former clients (self-proclaimed "nerds") view them as shady opportunists. Over time, Scott learned how to best deal with this select group's often unprincipled tactics and even became somewhat of an expert negotiator.

Through the years, Scott shared his candid wisdom with everyone who's worked for him, reached out, or those who seemed like they needed to learn this skill for themselves. People would tell him: "You should write a book!" And Scott thought so too.

A book was the best way to communicate his knowledge to the largest audience possible. A book would enable Scott to help more people, without the limitations of time and distance, fight against this group of, as he says, "unscrupulous" technical recruiters. He reasoned that if enough people working in IT knew how to assert themselves and demand fair pay, then maybe the whole industry would have to change for the better. It was an ambitious undertaking, but Scott knew a book would be the best shot at what he aimed to accomplish.

Scott was admittedly rather naïve about the whole process. Like most, he thought writing a book was a matter of sitting in front of the laptop and seamlessly having his thoughts appear. He was overseeing several different business ventures on top of raising a family with no spare time in between, but that didn't deter him. He reasoned that if a former children's author could quickly crank out the classic business fable *The One Minute Manager*, how hard could it really be?[1]

Turns out, *quite hard*—Scott sat disheartened with the project and ultimately only finished five pages of jumbled ideas. He knew the subject better than almost anyone; he had taught it to countless people. Yet, when it came to writing his experience down into a coherent chapter-by-chapter guide, he was stumped. How could this be?

Because writing, like public speaking, investing, or even playing golf, is an acquired skill that takes time

---

[1] Ken Blanchard, with the help of Spencer Johnson (author of New York Times bestseller *Who Moved My Cheese?*) wrote *The One Minute Manager* in 1982.

and study to develop. We can all write. We do it every day. But authoring a book is not like everyday writing. In fact, it's far from it.

There's a major difference between composing an email to a client and *professionally* writing to a wide audience on a specific subject with the intent of providing valuable information or expertise. This kind of writing is generally done by those who have dedicated a considerable amount of time and energy to learn, read, write, revise, and rewrite, until they are able to produce skillful works worth someone's time, interest, and hard-earned money. To put it simply, writing for an audience is a specialized skill some people spend their entire careers developing.

Scott is someone who does not readily accept defeat of any kind. He's stubborn to a fault and has had to learn some lessons the hard way. It took him two years before he was ready to admit that writing a book was not something he had the ability, skill, or time to do on his own.

That's when he reached out to Zoe, who ultimately became his co-writer. Her work has been published in magazines, featured on podcasts, and even produced by a theater company. Under a pseudonym, she has independently published multiple high-selling genre novels. Scott had the subject expertise, but Zoe had the knowledge, college degree, and experience with the entire start-to-finish publishing process.

Scott and Zoe started working together on the book in June of 2020. It was published in December and in its first week on Amazon, *A Nerd's Guide to Negotiating Salary and Benefits* ranked in the Top 5 for sales of newly-released business books. Scott was able to accomplish exactly what he set out to do: share his knowledge with as many relevant people as possible. And it was literally a dream come true.

If you think your brand is worth telling others about, you should write a book. If you have a unique experience, service, or product, you should write a book. If your expertise could benefit others, you should write a book. If you're still reading this, then you can probably sense you should need to write a book. Write it.

The best reason to write a nonfiction book is to share your knowledge or experience. If becoming published is one of your goals in life, do it to prove to yourself that *you can*. But if you're seeking to make money by selling thousands of books, the truth is, you're probably not going to succeed.

Failure is almost inevitable if book sales is your only goal. While the notion of making tens of thousands of dollars is incredibly appealing, the reality couldn't be more different since average book sales are shockingly small.

In a June 24th, 2020 article, "The 10 Awful Truths About Book Publishing," a Senior Editor at Berrett-Koehler Publishers referenced a BookScan analysis, which found that only 690 million print books were sold in the U.S. during 2019 (Piersanti).[2] The average U.S. book is now selling less than 200 copies per year and less than 1,000 copies over its lifetime.

Of those who do write, produce, publish, and market a book by themselves, very few will make a profit directly through book sales. Far fewer will earn enough to cover the time and money spent on creating the book in the first place. But, book sales are not a good way to measure the success of a nonfiction book.

In reality, a book about your brand can accomplish much for you. It establishes your authority, builds credibility, and attracts attention. Remember, writing a book is hard, and not everyone can do it—*that's exactly why it's so uniquely beneficial*. Having your name on the cover of a book distinguishes you as an expert in your field.

---

2   BookScan is an industry tracker of bookstore, online, and retail print book sales.

Being a published author can help promote your other endeavors. Validating your expertise and skills with a book can lead to opportunities that otherwise may never present themselves. A book can promote your product or service, attract clients, and even land speaking engagements. Everyone agrees that writing a book is an impressive accomplishment. A book will make you extraordinary and separate you from the competition. You may not make money from book sales, but you will make money from the attention your book can generate, *if* you leverage it.

Yes, sales are always nice. But the money earned from selling copies will pale in comparison to everything else you can gain. Once you realize what a book can help you accomplish, earning money through book sales will seem to be the very least of its potential benefits.

Our book will teach you how to both write and market a book. It encompasses everything from the planning, researching, and writing the first draft to the many rounds of editing, formatting, and design. It also offers an overview of the specifics of production, printing, and marketing. Our extensive experience with writing and publishing books has allowed us to identify and refine the complete process. If you're willing to put forth the time and energy into every step our book outlines, then you'll become a published author as well.

But, be forewarned: the actual process of writing a book can be arduous, seemingly overwhelming, and at times, even humbling. You must be willing to think of the process as an investment and act accordingly. However, with this book in hand and our expertise to guide you, your goal has never been more attainable.

PART I

BEFORE
YOU WRITE

CHAPTER 1
Setting the Foundation

It may sound contradictory, but you don't actually start writing a book by writing. There are several steps to complete before beginning the first draft, and you'll set yourself up for failure if you don't take the time to outline the book and create a writing plan.

Writing without an outline is like driving at night without headlights: you don't know where you're going and, eventually, it could end in disaster. In order to write about your brand so people will understand and gain value from it, it's imperative that you plan and organize your content into coherent, cohesive chapters that build upon your overall point for writing the book in the first place.

Before you create the outline, you need to establish some groundwork. This may seem a bit tedious, but keep in mind that this is quite literally the foundation of your book. If you don't take the time and make the effort to do this right, your book may never evolve.

So, the first thing you need to do is address the fundamentals, the thesis, and establish a working title (or a name you can attribute to your project). These three points form the basis of your book's plan. The planning of your book starts with defining its two fundamentals: its purpose and audience. This is often the most challenging part of the prewriting process, but once you have identified these elements, the remaining prep work tends to progress smoothly.

The first fundamental, the purpose, simply summarizes your reason for writing the book. What do you want your readers to gain from learning about your brand? Your purpose needs to be specific and of concrete value. If you don't specifically know the intent of your book or, for that matter, what defines your brand, neither will your readers.

Scott's purpose for writing his book was very specific; he was tired of IT professionals being vastly underpaid, and he wanted to teach them how to negotiate with technical recruiters to earn what they deserve. His purpose was succinct, its value was self-evident, and it focused on one specific issue within the IT industry. However, if he had tried to tackle all of the hiring issues in the industry, the book would have failed. Why?

Because having too broad of a scope typically results in a book covering too much surface-level information without going in depth on any of the topics. There's little value in a book that doesn't dive into a specific subject and provide the reader with insight they otherwise would not have gained.

Defining your book's purpose (while showcasing your brand) often subsequently leads to defining its audience as well. When you know exactly what your book is about, you usually know exactly who it is for.

Like your purpose, your audience has to be specific. As with your brand, your book will not appeal to everyone. Your defined purpose must be specific enough to exclude all but a very particular group of people who will find value in what you have to write. Your book's audience is akin to a customer persona— the imagined, ideal customer for your product or service. As you characterize your perceived audience, consider their unique perspective for why they would want to read your book. Take into account not just demographic elements, but also their values, motivations, fears—everything. Then, create a customer persona to determine who your audience is or should be.

Creating a customer persona is a must because your book is, like anything else being bought and sold, a product. And all products can't appeal to everyone: a self-employed rancher will not want to read your book about the benefits of a 403(b) Tax-Sheltered Annuity Plan. If you and your brand try to reach everyone, you'll probably miss who you actually want to target. But if you accurately determine your customer persona, you can understand your intended audience and who you need to write your book for. They are the people who can derive value from your book; hence, they are your potential readers and therefore matter the most.

In writing a book about how to best deal with technical recruiters, Scott's intended audience is smart but non-confrontational IT nerds who don't know how to negotiate. This group tends to fall in the demographic of 20-something, middle-income earners, but this is not the explicit audience, since not all 20-something, middle-income earners will need this book.

Consider the typical situation that someone would be in to want to read your book. They could be from different ages, ethnicities, economic backgrounds, etc., but share a common need that could be fulfilled by reading your book. That common need further defines your audience and can even shed light on your purpose for writing the book.

You can help identify your ambitions by asking yourself this: What do I hope to accomplish or gain by writing a book? Your goals should be specific and realistic. Are you hoping to attract clients? Do you want to distinguish yourself as an expert in your field? Increase brand awareness? Launch a speaking career? Garner publicity in the local or national news, be recognized in a trade journal, quoted in the mainstream media, or simply share your knowledge with others? Whatever your goals are, write them down and ensure they are within your ability to achieve. If you don't define them, you'll have nothing to judge your success against and will not be able to determine whether you reached them or not upon publication.

With the book's purpose and audience defined, the next step is to formulate its thesis. Your thesis should summarize the book's content and what makes your brand particular, while listing the features that distinguish it from others. But, how do you craft it to fit within your book?

We all remember having to write a thesis in school. This is a similar exercise, albeit more thorough than what a high school paper requires. A simple thesis statement in an essay goes something along the lines of: T*his is my topic/dilemma/anecdote and these are the points/examples/etc. that my essay will make.* Although that's elemental, it's a starting point.

The thesis should delineate all of the points you will present within the book and how they relate back to its purpose. It could range from one paragraph to one page in length, or sometimes more. Think of it as a simple synopsis that someone could use to understand what you're discussing even at the most basic level.

As you're an expert in your area, this exercise might be challenging since it can be difficult to simplify the depth of your knowledge. But, by being extremely specific to determine exactly what you want to write, you'll be able to create a chapter-by-chapter outline of everything you want to include—without becoming lost in your own thoughts and ideas.

Writing the thesis is a great litmus test to gauge whether you have enough content to write a book. It could even indicate if your content may be better suited for a series of short books or a collection of articles. Either, or both, of these options might ultimately serve your purpose for writing a book while helping you continuously build your brand, grow your business, and further your presence within your industry and beyond.

Preparing a first-rate thesis will allow you to organize your thoughts, experiences, and knowledge into a concise statement of your book's purpose. For example, let's say when you entered the business world, you had difficulty presenting yourself to colleagues. At first, you might focus on how you had struggled to create a professional image and couldn't seem to present your elevator pitch without stumbling over your words. These could all be aspects of the book, but it is not what the book is about. Rather, all of these components point to one common theme. Therefore, the thesis would be something along the lines of how to build your personal brand in a professional setting.

It's best to have a working title before the actual writing begins. Some writers and publishers would disagree with this, since you technically don't need a title until you're ready to publish. However, we recommend you choose a name for your book early on (you can always change it). This way, you can make sure that the title captures the essence of your brand and you'll be much more likely to complete the publishing process.

If you're seeking a shortcut to determining the name of your book, most good nonfiction titles tend to follow a format of a short but attention-grabbing title, followed by a longer subtitle that puts it into context.

Remember that this is a working title, not a representation of your final product. If you try to choose a final title before you begin writing, you may end up in a standstill agonizing over the best title before you can start the book. As you write, you'll likely settle on a decent placeholder title that reflects the book to come. You may never start—or finish—the book if you choose to wait until you have the "perfect" title. It's one of the ways that procrastination and perfectionism trick us into not actually working, and you can't let yourself fall for it.

The three hallmarks of an excellent title are that it does not do any harm, is something marketable, and alludes to your actual brand. What "not doing any harm" means is just that—don't choose a title that will turn potential readers away. If you pick an objectively poor title, it will make attracting readers much harder. A harmful title is best explained through examples. Let's go back to the book about establishing your personal brands. That could be valuable to a lot of people, right?

Here's how to destroy the book with a title and why:

> ✍ *How as a Young Professional I Tried to Make Lasting Network Connections at Events without Being Too Formal and Still Build My Personal Brand* Aside from being ridiculously long, it gives away the "secret sauce" of the book. Your book is essentially a solution to a reader's problem. If you tell them the answer on the front cover, why would they even bother reading it?

- ✍ *My Incredible Journey to Establishing Synergistic Business Relationships to Build My Top-Tier Personal Brand* An egotistical title is almost always inappropriate for nonfiction books, though there's plenty of stuffy books with titles like this. The biggest problem with this style is that it asserts the book to be grander and more epic than it could ever deliver. Furthermore, it's not a memoir, but the title would suggest otherwise. The people who probably should read it won't, and those who do may be disappointed or even confused.

- ✍ *How to Build Your Brand by Winning Friends and Influencing People* It's overly broad, of course, but that's not even the biggest issue with it. Ever heard of the classic work by Dale Carnegie? *How to Win Friends and Influence People* is a longtime bestseller and internationally-renowned book in the business world. And that's exactly the book that potential readers will think of when they see this title. There's almost nothing stopping you from giving your book the same name as other, more popular subjects. If someone buys your book expecting one thing but discovers another, that's annoying at best. At worst, you're flirting with potential fraud.

An excellent title must sell the book and provide an idea of what it's about without giving the whole story away. It's a tall order, but it can be accomplished. If you're seeking a shortcut to determining the name of your book, most good nonfiction titles tend to follow a format of a short but attention-grabbing title, followed by a longer subtitle that puts it into context. This way, your book will have a captivating short title and a subtitle that alludes to its content.

Using the traditional format, the title could be: *No Need to Hand Out Cards: A Young-Professional's Guide to Building Your Brand*. While the title could be better, it's catchy and states what the book is about. In a nutshell, if you spend some time playing around with this format, you're bound to come up with a title, or even several, that you'll like.

It's worth noting that Scott chose to include an expletive in the original title of his first book. Understandably, this has created some issues with mainstream publicity and probably prevented some sales. He also has had random people contact him just to criticize the provocative nature of the book. But here's the thing—Scott knew this would likely happen when he chose the title, and he accepted the possible consequences of his decision. He knew it would be controversial and anger some people, but he was committed to presenting his valuable knowledge so others could benefit. So, like him, entitle your book how you want, but consider all of the potential outcomes.

With these foundational elements out of the way, you're ready to move onto the outline.

SUMMARY

Before you write the outline, you need to establish the fundamentals of the book, the thesis, and a working title.

- The fundamentals are your purpose, target audience, and goals.

    - Purpose: Why are you writing the book?

    - Target Audience: Who is it for?

    - Goals: What do you hope to accomplish or gain?

- The thesis is a short summary of your book. You should be able to explain your subject in one sentence.

- A working title is recommended to help you own and commit to the project. Don't worry about choosing the final one.

    - A good title: does no harm, is marketable, and alludes to the content.

    - A good formula: a short and catchy title followed by a longer subtitle to put everything in context.

- If you have all of this established, you're ready to move onto the outline!

CHAPTER 2

Constructing the Outline

All of the prewriting work is important because it sets the stage for the creation of your book's outline. Like it or not, you must have an outline. The outline is quite literally the blueprint to your book. If you try to write without even a basic list of the chapters, you'll likely never complete it. And if you somehow manage to, chances are that it won't be your best work.

Defining the purpose, target audience, and goals leads to the thesis. Writing the thesis leads to writing the synopsis, which leads to constructing the outline, which will eventually turn into your manuscript (which is then edited, proofed, formatted, and published as your book).

Your synopsis, which is generally a one to two-page overview of your book and detailed enough that someone can fully grasp your book (and hence, your brand) just by reading it, should list all of the points you will present. These points, which will serve as chapters, can be organized chronologically or by importance, relevance, gut feel—whatever makes sense for your specific book.

Some people approach a nonfiction book as a longform essay and structure it accordingly. This means presenting the central thesis in the introduction, developing the major points into chapters, and then affirming those points in the conclusion. However, this is just one form.

There's also the "class" method, which is used in a variety of nonfiction books. The chapters are structured into lessons that expand on one point to the next in order to teach or convey the overall thesis. You can think of this configuration similar to a PowerPoint presentation used to teach a lesson. If you're trying to specifically explain something to your reader, this might be the best method.

Another method is to break your synopsis into a list of bullet points, and then organize them into groups of relevant sections. From there, you can often sense how the chapters should emerge.

Ultimately, the configuration just needs to "flow" and your chapters need to "fit" together. These are clearly subjective terms, so while an outside perspective can help guide you, only you can really determine whether the arrangement is working. If after finishing the first draft you find that the chapters don't evolve in the best order, then content can always be shifted. However, mastering the chapter configuration during this stage will save a lot of time later during the revision process.

Most nonfiction books generally follow this structure:

- ✍ An introduction that presents the purpose, establishes your qualifications, and provides a broad overview.

- ✍ A series of chapters that describes the points of the purpose and builds on the information presented.

- ✍ A conclusion that summarizes and reiterates your chapters. You may also want to utilize the closing section for any relevant self-promotion.

Bring your readers along just as you would a prospective client. Then, make sure you detail the aspects of what distinguishes you or your brand that they might not know.

Each chapter traditionally begins with an initial sentence or two of what it's about, and then presents a more detailed overview. If your book involves subjects the average person may not be familiar with, you'll want to work your way up to the more complex topics. Walk before you run—you may be an expert in the subject, but your readers might be picking up your book to learn about you, your product, or your expertise for the first time. Bring them along just as you would a prospective client. Then, make sure you detail the aspects of what distinguishes you or your brand that your reader might not know. From there, segueway into what makes you unique.

Most readers tend to retain information and understand a concept better when there is a narrative to augment the information being presented. With this in mind, you may want to review your chapter outlines and identify where you can include anecdotes. So long as they are relevant and contribute to what the book discusses, short stories, quick tales, and recollections often work as great chapter openers, examples, case studies, or transitions to different topics. Readers respond to stories and if you choose yours right, anecdotes will greatly enhance your book.

A good anecdote can help validate a real-life key point, show the consequence of a problem presented, depict a lesson in action, or express a relevant experience. It can help readers relate to and reinforce what you are presenting. However, don't throw a story in only because it's funny, personal, or just something you feel like sharing. If your chosen anecdote doesn't help establish a specific point, it will only be distracting.

The best way to promote your brand or company in a way that can build your point is to include experiential anecdotes. What do you or your company do especially well that you can provide as an example for what you're discussing in the book?

Since a goal of being published is to promote your brand, we caution you not to be blatant about it. Self-promotion is understandable, but it needs to be warranted and conducive to your original purpose for writing a book. It's the same with the anecdotes—if it won't help make your point, it may detract from your credibility and diminish the reader's trust.

The best way to promote your brand or company in a way that can build your point is to include experiential anecdotes. What do you or your company do especially well that you can provide as an example for what you're discussing in the book? These uncommon illustrations are effective additions to your book, and they can prompt the reader to trust or become interested in you.

An applicable example is this book; it's intended to teach others how to write and publish a book in order to build their brand (and in many cases generate additional opportunities). However, we recognize that for some people, publishing a book requires more time than they can commit. Or, perhaps they do not have the skill or interest to do it themselves.

We suggest that you adopt the same principle with your book—don't try to push the reader to become a client. Rather, present your story and gain their potential interest as a byproduct.

There's no ideal number of chapters required to produce a complete book. The number needed is as many as it takes to fully express your purpose with supporting points. Typically, a nonfiction book will consist of five to twenty chapters. If your outline falls under or exceeds this range, make sure there is a specific reason. If it's too short, you may be missing content. If it's too long, you may have enough content for two books.

Similarly, there's no ideal word count, but there is a usual number. The typical range for business books is between 25,000 and 40,000 words. You might need more or less to convey what you want to share, but there may be a lot of fluff to cut if a first draft exceeds 40,000 words.

In comparison, most novels are usually more than 50,000 words. Works of fiction need this length to establish the characters and setting, build conflict, create narrative arcs, and lay the general prose and imagery. A business book doesn't require any of these elements and can cover more information in fewer words.

A succinct approach to your points may lead to a better outcome. You're hoping that readers will choose to make an investment of their time (and usually money) to read what you're working so hard to write. So, you don't want to risk being wordy and losing their interest. However, this is more of a consideration during the editing process.

An outline is not the end of the planning stage. Before you can move on to actually writing your book, you need to establish the writing plan. That's next.

SUMMARY

- Before constructing an outline, write a synopsis by expanding on your thesis.

    - Your synopsis should be one to two pages and detailed enough that anyone can grasp your book by reading it.

- Utilize your synopsis to create an outline in one of three ways:

    - The "essay" method, which presents the central thesis in the introduction, develops the major points into chapters, and affirms this in the conclusion.

    - The "class" method, which structures chapters like lessons that expand on one point to the next.

    - The "bullet point" method that breaks your synopsis into points which are organized into groups of relevant sections from which chapters emerge.

- Most nonfiction books include:

    - An introduction to present the purpose, establish your qualifications, and provide a broad overview.

- Chapters that describe the points of the purpose and build on the information presented.

- A conclusion to reiterate the chapters and present relevant self-promotion.

- Anecdotes should be relevant and enrich the content.

- There's no ideal chapter or word count.

PART II

THE
WRITING

CHAPTER 3
Establishing a Writing Plan

You've determined your book's purpose and its content. To speak in metaphors, you've drafted detailed blueprints for what will be a great house. But if you don't set a construction schedule, that house will never be built.

You're unlikely to write your book if you don't set and follow a specific schedule. You can't "wait for inspiration to strike" or trust yourself to write intermittently. No matter whether the words are flowing or you're struggling to craft each sentence, writing is *work*. Luckily, the battle is restricted to planning and committing to a time to sit yourself down to work. Once you're there, productivity is almost always inevitable.

There are several different types of writing schedules to choose from. The best one for you depends on your time commitment, availability, lifestyle, and preferences. We'll describe a few, but the best schedule is ultimately the one that works for you. So long as you stick to it, there's no wrong way to do the work.

The first option is to pick a specific time of the day to write. This could be every day from 9 am to 11 am, 12:30 pm to 1 pm, 11:45 pm to 12 am, whatever is manageable and fits your routine. When you decide what time out of your day that you'll spend writing, you're more likely to make it a part of your daily routine. Eventually, your brain may even become "cued" to be creative and productive during this time. This type of schedule works best for those who need a set schedule or have a predictable day-to-day routine.

Schedules only work if you can trust yourself to stick to them. If you're someone who needs to have pressure to produce, whether real or self-imposed, your best bet may be to give yourself different deadlines to ensure that you hit every milestone.

If your schedule varies or you require flexibility for when you can write, you may want to set a certain number of hours per week rather than specific times. You may decide to dedicate ten hours per week to the project. That could mean three hours one day, two the next, half an hour on the third day, and then four and a half hours over the weekend to meet your goal. So long as you stick to your weekly quota, you can give yourself a lot of leeway with when and how long you write.

Another preferred method is to set a word count for each week or writing session. This way, you're setting goals for yourself that ensure progress rather than focusing on the time spent in front of the screen. Ideally, a word count goal forces you to write rather than stare at a blank screen, and it can help reduce procrastination.

You might stick to your schedule of sitting down to write, but typing and cutting and pasting a few sentences during that time won't produce a first draft. Many people fall into the perfectionist's trap of working to create one perfect paragraph before they can move on to the next one. In reality, your first draft won't be perfect regardless of the hours you spend on it. But you have to type the draft to be able to edit and make it better.

Schedules only work if you can trust yourself to stick to them. If you're someone who needs to have pressure to produce, whether real or self-imposed, your best bet may be to give yourself different deadlines to ensure you hit every milestone. If you give yourself until the end of every month to complete a chapter, you may not end up writing until then. But whether you're writing one paragraph a day or the whole thing the night before, you're still making progress, and that's ultimately all that matters.

The point of a writing schedule is to commit the time to just do it. You might work for fifteen minutes a day or a fifteen-hour stretch every month. But if you're actually writing and making progress, how you arrange your time doesn't matter.

Some first-time writers believe they need a set place to write along with a specific schedule. Regardless, the best place to work is where you can focus. While some people need a place devoid of distractions, others need background noise to keep their minds from drifting.

Wherever you can concentrate best is where you should write, but it never hurts to break the monotony and try someplace new. We all have our unique "best" setup and through trial and error, you'll eventually learn what yours is.

A writing schedule is not all you need to ensure you make progress on writing your book. An accountability plan is just as important. Next, we'll address how to create a method to hold yourself accountable.

SUMMARY

- You're unlikely to write your book if you don't set and stick to a specific schedule.

- A writing plan will specify when, where, and how you will actually write. The best specific plan for you will depend on your schedule and personal factors.

- Different writing plans include:

    - A scheduled recurring day and time.

    - A weekly or monthly quota of hours.

    - A weekly or monthly word count goal.

- Some people may need to establish a set writing place alongside a writing time.

- The most important part of any writing plan is to stick to it.

CHAPTER 4
Setting an Accountability Plan

Implementing and following a writing plan should lead to the completion of your book. But devising and sticking to an accountability plan will nearly guarantee that you follow-through with your goals. Like other major life goals, writing a book is something a lot of people want to do, even plan to do, but still somehow fail to accomplish it.

Think about how quickly most people's New Year's resolutions unravel; a Forbes article found that approximately 80% of resolutions get abandoned in or around February.[3] The year starts and someone says they want to lose weight. They pick a diet and exercise plan. Then, they buy workout clothes, sneakers, fresh produce, meal prep containers, everything. They pack kale salads for lunch. They even set their alarms an hour early to hit the gym before work. They've done everything to set the stage to lose weight and seem determined to achieve their goal.

But by February, they are back to their old ways. Why? Because although they were committed to the preparation, people often fail to keep themselves accountable with a daily routine and measurable progress.

---

3   Murphy, Mark, "This is the Month When New Year's Resolutions Fail—Here's How to Save Them." Forbes, 2019.

There are different ways to hold yourself accountable. Like a writing schedule, there is no single right way.

Sharing goals makes a person more likely to accomplish them because verbalizing plans creates a "social pressure" to perform. The threat of a potential embarrassment can be stressful, but effective. A little stress is actually good since it can help maintain motivation.

There are different techniques to hold yourself accountable. Like a writing schedule, there is no single right way. But one surefire method is to share your intent to write a book; how public you are with this is entirely up to you. Some prefer to broadcast their plan by making social media posts or telling everyone they know. This works best if you need public pressure to be productive. It can also help generate future interest in your book, as these same people may eventually become your first readers.

However, if you'd prefer not to tell the whole world, you might consider picking one specific person to confide in and ask that they periodically check in on your progress. Select someone whom you hold in high regard, since you're likely to be more motivated to not disappoint them. When making your request, confirm that your trusted individual is comfortable with assuming the role. Some people may not like the responsibility, while others may be excited to support you and your writing endeavors.

If you'd prefer to hold yourself solely accountable and not share your ambition with anyone, you may want to establish a private reward system for hitting certain milestones. When you finish a chapter, you could take yourself out for a steak dinner, buy the new suit or purse you've been eyeing, or end the day early to play a round of golf. Giving yourself permission to indulge in something may be what ultimately motivates you to complete your book.

Some people are of the mindset that not telling others about their project before it's done is better. Their reasoning is that sharing their intent can give them a "premature sense of achievement," and thus, they'll be less likely to complete it. In reality, all that matters is having a plan that best meets your schedule, matches your work habits, and aligns with your motivation style. This is the key to completing your book.

SUMMARY

✎ To maintain their motivation to write a book, many people need to establish both accountability and writing plans.

✎ There are three typical accountability plans:

 📖 Broadcasting your intent to others and creating a "social pressure" situation to perform.

 📖 Choosing a person to confide in and having them periodically check in to ask about your progress.

 📖 Establishing a private reward system for hitting certain milestones.

CHAPTER 5
Conducting Research

At this point, you've established your book's purpose and audience, the information you intend to cover, and how you plan to follow through with your writing. But reflect back to your term paper days for a moment: after settling on a thesis and before you could start writing, what was always the next step? The process of *conducting research*.

You may be an expert in your field and can draw on years of experience, but even with your credentials, you'll most likely need to gather additional sources and support your points. The outside information you include will validate what you're saying, corroborate your experiences, and increase the book's value for your readers.

Ensuring what you state is true and substantiated will protect and even legitimize your brand. Your end goal is to produce a high-quality book that offers value to your readers. Fact-checking your content and referencing credible sources will ensure value for your readers and distinguish your book as a high-quality product.

If you present something as fact and it turns out to be inaccurate or otherwise untrue, it will reflect poorly on you, damage your credibility, and tarnish your brand. At the very least, it may cost you some business, or worse, all the professional opportunities afforded to published authors.

Established authors who have a relationship with a traditional publishing house often have a team to fact-check their work for them. But if you're following the independent or Do-It-Yourself route to publishing, the onus is on *you* to ensure the accuracy of information and protect your credibility.

While tedious, incorporating reputable references is standard practice and adds immeasurable value and credibility to your book. This is especially important as a first-time author or as a relatively unknown expert in your field.

Given the vastness of the internet, the amount of information at your fingertips can be staggering. However, exercising excellent research techniques will help you find quality information more quickly.

Basic practices include:

- ✎ Vary your search engine.

- ✎ Simplify your search term or phrase. Less words usually equate to less erroneous results.

- ✎ Use quotation marks around a specific word or phrase that *must* be included. For instance, keying in Catskills will also produce results for cats and skills, but "Catskills" will only collect results about the town in southeast New York.

- ✍ Remove unhelpful words. Searching "editing -video" will produce editing results, but will exclude any mention of the practice of video editing.

- ✍ Focus on more reputable sources. Use sites that end in .org, .gov and .edu.

As you conduct your research, it's best to keep your notes organized in a document separate from your manuscript. This way, you can refer to and copy-and-paste information without potentially muddling all of the content. This practice is helpful when you cite your sources—you won't waste time scrolling through your browser history if your notes include a URL to the article. You'll save yourself time later during the writing phase by being organized now.

As you write, you'll need to find the right balance between presenting your experiences and supplementing them with information from outside sources. Some of this balance correlates to your reason for writing your book. Since you're writing to educate readers on your expertise and to boost your business, the majority of the book will concentrate on your know-how. Your personal snapshot of your field and acumen are exclusive. But if you reference industry metrics, explain the practices of competitors, or claim a special recognition or achievement, you need to support these statements with objective facts.

General statements are a different story. A general statement could be made that independent publishing is on the rise in the United States, without identifying any sources. However, if we claim that in 2011, independently-published titles outnumbered the traditionally-published market at nearly 2:1, we need to credit author Justine Tal Goldberg for this information from her article, *"200 Million Americans Want to Publish Books, But Can They?"* (Goldberg).

While tedious, incorporating reputable references is standard practice and adds immeasurable value and credibility to your book. This is especially important as a first-time author or as a relatively unknown expert in your field. A book should boost your reputation and enhance your brand's image, and including trustworthy sources will ensure that.

Be aware of setting up yourself in a predicament. Specifically, if you delay your writing or revisions for "research purposes," you could spend months or years belaboring the process and making very little progress on your writing. Identify the points that require additional information or supporting facts and then take the required steps—or, enlist someone who can perform the task for you.

If you're in the middle of the writing process and need to conduct supporting research, simply insert "TK" into the sentence and keep your writing flowing. (The worst thing you can do is to interrupt your progress every few paragraphs.) Since there are very few words with the letters "TK" next to each other, using the *command+f* keyboard shortcut, you can later search for the spots in your manuscript that require fact-finding and find them with minimal effort.

With the fundamentals of the book established and both a writing and accountability plan in hand, you can proceed to the book writing stages.

SUMMARY

- You'll most likely need to draw on research to gather additional sources and support your book's points.

- If you present something as fact and it turns out to be inaccurate or otherwise untrue, it will reflect poorly on you, damage your credibility, and tarnish your brand.

- Exercising excellent research techniques will help you find quality information more quickly.

- As you conduct your research, it's best to keep your notes organized in a document separate from your manuscript.

- If you delay your writing or revisions for "research purposes," you could spend months or years belaboring the process and making very little progress on your writing.

PART III

THE
MANUSCRIPT

CHAPTER 6
Composing Your First Draft

Writing a first draft of your manuscript is one of the major aspects of publishing a book. As you begin the writing process, don't be surprised if the initial manuscript evolves into a vastly different completed book. The first draft is often called a "rough draft" for exactly that reason—it will be far removed from your finished product. Your first draft will require some trimming, smoothing out, bolstering, and a myriad of large and small edits. In fact, the editing process can often take longer than the writing process itself, especially if this is your first book.

Unless you're a clandestine genius, your first draft is probably not going to be very good. Since it requires countless hours of time and determination to complete, you'll want to make all your efforts worthwhile by producing a manuscript that reflects your best work. Therefore, you'll need to dedicate even more energy into editing what you've written.

Before you reach that point, we recommend taking a break from the project entirely. Stepping away from your first draft will provide you with a fresh perspective and renewed energy. However, you might think this is counterintuitive. If you have all of this work ahead of you, why put it off? If you have momentum, why stop now?

At this juncture, your focus is probably waning and you may be too locked-in with what you've written so far. Your frame of mind won't be conducive to editing your book. Taking time off after completing the first draft is vital to preventing burnout and will allow you to return to the project with "fresh" eyes.

There's no right amount of time to take off. Less than a week may not be enough, and anything more than a month could make returning to the project difficult. Find a window of time that allows you to recharge without losing sight of your end goal, and return to your book when you feel ready to make revisions.

SUMMARY

- The first draft of your manuscript will require a myriad of edits and the process can often take longer than the actual writing itself.

- Taking a break from the project prior to editing will provide you with a fresh perspective and renewed energy.

CHAPTER 7
Enduring the Read-Through

A read-through is just that—reading everything you've written. Since we're all our worst critics, a read-through may be painful or challenging, especially since you may not remember your rationale for why you crafted a paragraph a certain way, included a particular anecdote, or arranged your chapters in that order. After your time away, you'll be able to gain an overall sense of how your manuscript reads at this stage.

It's hard to do this by yourself, but a read-through is the start of understanding what needs to be addressed to improve your first draft.

Ideally, a review of your draft will present you with an opportunity to objectively review your manuscript, identify what you need to work on, and isolate what's not working at all. It's hard to do this by yourself, but a read-through is the start of understanding what needs to be addressed to improve your first draft.

The norm is to perform two read-throughs. The first time, your intent is to read solely for understanding the content. Try to think from the perspective of a reader. Imagine they don't know about you, your business, or your brand. Does the included information present everything necessary to understand your story and communicate what distinguishes you? If not, mark what's missing or what you need to clarify or expand on. You'll address the specific changes later.

As you continue to read, where does the material seem confusing, excessive, or irrelevant? Is the nomenclature too complicated? Are the multiple pages detailing the history of your company too long? Is the sidestory about suffering through bankruptcy and a failed partnership reinforcing a key point of the book? If not, make a note and revisit any dilemas later.

The second read-through should focus on the prose, or the actual writing itself. Reading your entire draft aloud during this step is essential. It will allow you to hear the tone of your words and better determine where any given content doesn't flow or seems to repeat itself. Again, mark up any of these sections to address later.

It's prudent to forgo making any actual changes to your first draft until you conclude the second read-through. To keep your edits organized, take notes on either a separate document or notebook and jot down any thoughts or possible changes you have in mind as you read. Even seemingly miniscule ideas and impressions may prove to be incredibly helpful during your first revision.

While you should take as many notes as you can, it's important to keep your hands off the draft during this stage so you don't accidentally jump into the editing stage too soon. If you begin to edit before you complete the read-through, you may end up making edits now that aren't helpful after you read the rest of the draft. The read-through is for getting a holistic sense of the state of your draft; once you understand where it's at in its entirety, you can then go back and make the necessary changes.

SUMMARY

- ✍ The read-through allows you to attain an overall sense of how your manuscript reads at this stage.

- ✍ You should complete two read-throughs of the first draft.

  - ▢ The first is to read solely for understanding the content.

  - ▢ The second should focus on the prose, or the actual writing itself.

- ✍ Don't make any edits during either step. Instead, mark the draft and make notes to use during the editing process.

CHAPTER 8
Tackling the First Revision

Making the first revision to your manuscript is like making a tackle in football. You know it may be painful, but you need to believe you can do it, and you have to keep your head up (otherwise, you risk breaking your neck).

Reviewing what you've written and determining how you can make it better is not always easy. While the first revision won't be the only one, it will be the start to greatly improving your draft. After completing the read-through process, the revision won't be too bad. And keep in mind, it will only make your manuscript better.

You can't depend on your skills alone to ensure the book is error-free. At this point, your manuscript needs the help of outside input and advice.

The first step is to copy the original document and paste it into an entirely new one. Name this document "Revision 1" or whatever makes it clear that this is your first revision. Each iteration of your manuscript should be in a separate and easily identifiable document. Never make your first round edits in the same version; it's important to save all of the earlier drafts, including the original. By following this practice, it will be easier to track the manuscript's development and it allows you to revert back to the original text if necessary.

Focus on one paragraph or section at a time and utilize the notes you previously compiled as your guide. To begin, fix any issues with the technical parts of the book. That means the grammar, syntax, diction, sentence structure, and semantics—everything to do with how the words connect. Next, make the content edits as marked, which could involve rewriting a series of paragraphs, or even an entire chapter.

Finally, make edits based on the flow of the book. This process is more objective and intuitive than the others. The goal is to ensure your manuscript "sounds" right and it's best accomplished by again reading the draft aloud. Then, as needed, recompose what you've written until it's clear and can be understood by your readers.

Completing the revision process doesn't mean that your manuscript is done—you're far from the finish line. While the revised draft is undoubtedly better than the first, it's still a work-in-progress and is not ready to take to the printer quite yet. You can't depend on your skills alone to ensure the book is error-free. At this point, your manuscript needs the help of outside input and advice.

SUMMARY

✍ Reviewing what you've written and determining how you can make it better is not always easy, but it's necessary for improving the draft.

✍ Before making any edits, copy and paste your current draft into a new document. Save every new iteration of the draft in separate files.

✍ Based on the notes you took during the read-through, edit for content first and then for flow.

✍ Ensuring your manuscript "sounds" right is best accomplished by reading the draft aloud.

✍ Completing the revision process doesn't mean your manuscript is done; you will now need outside help as well.

CHAPTER 9

Enlisting an Editor

The value of an editor cannot be overstated. Quality editors aren't free, unless you personally know someone who possesses the qualifications and will complete the job as a favor. However, be wary. A good editor should not be your close friend since they need to be objective and be able to offer honest criticism. If you want to produce a quality book that will distinguish you and help build your credibility and brand, you'll want an editor who can significantly improve your writing.

Your editor will not only revise and enhance your manuscript where needed, but they'll also offer commentary as they see fit. An acquaintance or someone with a low price point is unlikely to fulfill that duty to the degree that it needs to be done.

An editor is not paid to spare your feelings or stroke your ego. You may not like all or some of their input, but their contributions will make your book better.

The editor's job is to point out flaws, offer suggestions, identify where references need to be included, cut or expand content, and share any major concerns they may have. An excellent editor's work is comprehensive, and their expertise and objectivity is crucial to improving your manuscript.

An editor is not paid to spare your feelings or stroke your ego. You may not like some of their input, but their contributions will make your book better. They may propose that a certain anecdote, example, or entire section needs drastic improvement or even to be cut completely. Their edits may sting. But, it's an indispensable part of the publishing process that *will* improve your manuscript.

You should enlist the services of a well-qualified editor if you:

- Have the funds to hire one. (If not, you may want to suspend your project until you do.)

- Want to best showcase your expertise and level of professionalism by producing a well-written book with high-quality content.

- Recognize the benefits of utilizing a specialist who can provide their own proficiency.

- Are self-confident and able to accept criticism while being open to suggestions and an outside opinion.

- Concede that being unwavering and resolutely committed to your writing style will not produce your best work.

- Accept that improving your draft at this stage will ultimately enhance your brand's message.

- ✍ Want to produce a high-quality book that will distinguish you and help build your credibility and brand.

- ✍ Are having difficulty grasping the intricacies of the book-writing process and want direction from a seasoned ally.

The determining factor of hiring an editor should be based on your original purpose for writing a book. For instance, if you are writing it for just your family and friends to document your life and cement your legacy, then you may not need an editor. But if you intend to release your book to a wider audience, then it's in your best interest to work with an editor.

Finding a qualified editor is dependent upon what you're willing to spend. If your resources are limited, you may want to seek a freelance editor. Keep in mind that a low price may mean an inexperienced editor with an insufficient portfolio and possibly limited or no background in your subject matter.

Furthermore, since many of the least expensive editors are not based in the United States and live all over the world, there could be a language barrier, or at the very least, a difference in dialect or vernacular. As for pricing, a common practice is to advertise a steep online discount for their services, especially if you complete a brief questionnaire or click on a link for more information. Remember, you'll get what you pay for.

If you elect to hire a freelance editor, be sure to check every prospective candidate's portfolio of past work to get a sense of whether they're suited for your project. Conduct a virtual meeting to determine if there could be any potential communication obstacles. You've already put in the work and energy to write the book, so hiring an experienced editor to guide the manuscript into a high-quality final product is just the finishing touch.

SUMMARY

- ✍ To produce a quality book that will distinguish you and help build your credibility and brand, you'll want an editor who can improve your writing.

- ✍ A proven professional will provide expertise and experience, and have the ability to be objective.

- ✍ Seemingly inexpensive freelancers may have an insufficient portfolio and possibly limited or no experience with your subject matter.

- ✍ If you elect to hire a freelance editor, be sure to conduct a virtual meeting to determine if there could be any potential communication obstacles.

CHAPTER 10
Finding Beta Readers

The function of a beta reader is not as universally known as the role of an editor, but they're nearly as important in the publishing process since they provide multiple benefits to an author. Unlike an editor, beta readers don't require any formal expertise or qualifications; conversely, that's why they can be such an invaluable asset. In the proverbial sense, they help a writer, especially first-time ones, see the wood for the trees.

As you begin your next round of edits, beta readers provide you with their notes, opinions, and suggestions to make adjustments, as well as specific feedback such as where a section may be too verbose or contain flowery language.[1] They can even offer input on the organization and layout of the chapters. You might find beta readers to be overly critical; they'll tell you what they like and what they don't. However, you decide what feedback to incorporate or disregard.

Beta readers essentially serve as a test audience before your book is published and offer critiques of your manuscript. Their job is not to make corrections. Rather, they share their overall impressions and their

---

1   When you share your manuscript with outside parties, such as beta readers, send it as a PDF file via email. For added security, you can make the document password-protected and only available for a limited period of time.

insight as to why you might want to make a specific change to any aspects of your manuscript.

The best readers are those who would organically read your book and whom you don't personally know. Friends and family are not ideal candidates for the role because they're unlikely to provide the honest feedback your book will need to improve.

If you have a particular question in mind or a section you can't seem to phrase correctly, you can ask beta readers to assess certain elements or the manuscript as a whole. They can tell you if your writing matches your brand messaging. They can also share if they can readily distinguish what makes your product or service unique.

Weigh beta reader feedback as you complete your final revisions and take into consideration if you received repeated feedback about the same issue. If a suggestion can improve the narrative, make it. For the suggestions that don't seem to fit or are irrelevant, disregard or discuss them with your editor.

Beta readers are not literary professionals and your potential audience likely isn't either. Your book is a product, and beta readers will sample it before it goes to market. Although you want to have a diverse group of participants, it's ideal to have members who fit within your book's target audience. The best ones are those who would organically read your book and whom you don't personally know. Friends and family are not ideal candidates for the beta reader role because they're unlikely to provide the honest feedback your book will need to improve.

A variety of websites are used to connect authors and beta readers, including specialized Facebook groups and subreddits (a forum dedicated to a specific topic on Reddit). The selection process usually involves making a post on any one of these sites, receiving responses, and selecting those who appear qualified and well-suited for the book's topic.

While beta reader contributions can help make a good book great, not every author utilizes their services as part of their writing process. This may be due to personal preference, being overly confident in their writing and not wanting to receive any sort of feedback, or because of the associated cost. Generally, in exchange for providing their services, beta readers are given a free copy of the book upon its publication.

However, many beta readers require some sort of negotiated payment. With either arrangement, there's no guarantee of attracting suitable respondents who represent the proper demographics and have the bonafide skills, time, and integrity to do the job right.

While it's illegal for a beta reader to steal your work due to intellectual property rights, there is always the risk that they may take or otherwise appropriate your ideas, concepts, or any original material presented within your manuscript. If this does happen, there's not much you can do beyond entering a costly and long legal battle that offers no guarantee of settlement. Selecting a reputable service can prevent this outcome while still providing the quality feedback needed to ready your draft for final revisions.

Beta readers can help guide your revisions through the viewpoint of a reader rather than an editor. While their inexpert feedback may not always be helpful, their insight as an average reader can prove incredibly valuable for tailoring your book to its target audience.

SUMMARY

- Beta readers act as the test group for your manuscript.

- They can provide you with their notes, opinions, or suggestions to make adjustments.

- Take into consideration if the majority of readers identify a common issue.

- As objective reviewers within your target audience that you don't know personally, they can provide specific and honest feedback.

- Participants can be found on a variety of Internet sites that serve as matchmakers. However:

  - Many require some sort of payment.

  - There's no guarantee of attracting suitable respondents who have the bonafide skills, time and integrity to do the job right.

  - Although it's illegal to steal your work, there is always the risk that a beta reader may take your ideas, concepts, or any material in your manuscript.

CHAPTER 11
Making Final Revisions

Although the writing process concludes with the final round of revisions, a number of steps are involved before you can put your manuscript "to bed." Steps include: incorporating your editor's recommendations, considering your beta readers' feedback, and adding or revising any content. Any changes you make can be sent to your editor and even beta readers for their review, but ideally, these revisions should be the last ones you'll make. Once these steps are taken, your manuscript should be complete.

A first time author could end up in a perfectionist's trap of making endless insignificant edits, fine-tuning words, and completing limitless rewrites.

It's not easy to determine if your writing is finished, the editing is sufficient, and the content is complete. There's no established timeline or end date and, unlike other disciplines, writing a book doesn't necessarily have objective endpoints. There's no clear line to cross that advances a manuscript to a book.

Thus, a first time author could end up in a perfectionist's trap of making endless insignificant edits, fine-tuning words, and completing limitless rewrites. These changes may not be "wrong," but they may obstruct the book's completion. Giving your manuscript "just one more look" will always reveal some detail that could be improved. At some point, making revisions stops being productive and can even weaken your content or delivery.

To get the best sense of how your writing reads, remember to read your final manuscript aloud. This time, listen for continuity problems and ask yourself if the content drives the book forward and will compel your audience to keep reading. Remember as you review your work that writing is an art and art is subjective. If you want to create something *good*, then you must accept that you will never write the perfect book. As Leonardo Da Vinci said: "Art is never finished, only abandoned."

There comes a point when it's hard to know if you've crossed the finish line; rather, you have to *decide* that you are finished writing your manuscript and rely on your instinct to reach this conclusion. Other times, this decision may be out of your hands because of a deadline. You may have more you want to share, but that content may be better suited for another book rather than cramming it into this one.

You can't wait for when you and any confidants, including editors and beta readers, can't find anything else to improve because that point will never come. The best way to decide if your manuscript is complete is by asking yourself: *"Have I done my best to present a clear and complete message that will benefit my readers, while building my brand and distinguishing myself as an expert?"* If you can honestly answer "yes," then your manuscript is ready to become a book.

SUMMARY

- The final revision is the stage of editing where you incorporate feedback from your editor and beta readers and add any final thoughts you may have.

- There's no clear finish line to cross that advances a manuscript into a book.

- You have to **decide** that you are finished writing your manuscript, and sometimes you just need to rely on your instinct to reach this conclusion.

PART IV

FROM MANUSCRIPT TO BOOK

CHAPTER 12

Calculating a Production Budget

Although the writing steps are complete, the publishing process is far from over. The next steps have little to do with writing. Rather, they focus on the technical publishing steps that most first-time authors and the general public aren't familiar with.

Once your book's content has been written, edited, and reviewed, it may seem there's little else required to have it printed and distributed. However, these steps are critical if you're seeking to present the world with a book that establishes you as an author, distinguishes you as a published expert in your field, and helps build your brand.

Continuing this endeavor requires moving beyond the writing process and into the production operation. You'll need to create a production budget for an assortment of expenses. Books have different production formats (i.e. paperback, hardcover, digital, and audio), distribution sources, and marketing channels to choose from. These options require funds that most first-time authors may not have anticipated, and many of these steps require time and expertise that many new authors lack.

If your book will act as an extension of your brand, then the content and production should reflect this.

The production budget will directly correlate to your goals for producing your book; your defined end goal will be indicative of whether you need to hire skilled professionals to complete some of the steps or if you can manage the work yourself.

For instance, if your book will act as an extension of your brand, you'll want to utilize the services of a highly-skilled graphic designer to produce the front and back covers. Together, you can create covers that best project your company's image and message, and further your brand awareness. If you intend to educate your readers regarding a unique service or product, you'll likely rely on visual aids to communicate the information. Most people aren't artistic and tech-savvy enough to produce the high-quality illustrations, complicated graphics, and text excerpts needed for your book. Instead, you'll want to enlist the expertise of an experienced formatter.

Some books will require a great deal of data and statistics, which take time to gather. Many authors could benefit from contracting a researcher, or a writing assistant who can conduct, transcribe, and edit interviews. At the least, your production budget should include money to hire a proofreader, and maybe even a copyeditor.

Depending on the resources and attention allocated to marketing, whether individually or through the work of publicity professionals, your book can create opportunities for you and your business that you may never have anticipated. However, it would be imprudent to expect the book sales of a first-time author will generate enough net revenue to cover its production costs, let alone pay you for the time required to write it. And if you intend to distribute free copies to prospects, clients, influencers, and the media, as well as friends and family, you need to factor this expense and potential shipping costs into your post-production, distribution budget.

Remember, your book is an investment into your brand and business. While you may not make profit directly through book sales, there is a wealth of opportunities available to authors that you will be able to access with your book. If you leverage it correctly, your book will "pay off" in many other ways.

SUMMARY

- A production budget refers to the professional services required to complete the technical aspects of your book.

- A highly-skilled graphic designer can produce both front and back covers that best project your company's brand.

- If a great deal of data and statistics will be needed, you may want to contract a researcher, or a writing assistant who can conduct, transcribe, and edit interviews.

- Actual book sales will most likely not generate enough net revenue to cover the production costs, but it will pay off in other ways.

CHAPTER 13
Utilizing a Copy Editor and Proofreader

Writing and publishing a book is not a solo journey. The writing itself may be, but the final steps of the publishing process require outside review and feedback to ensure a high-quality final product. Beta readers often provide feedback from the mindset of the audience, such as confusing content, disjointed concepts, and awkward phrasing. A copy editor focuses on the technical, making revisions as they thoroughly review your manuscript's content.

A copy editor is an investment worth consideration. A general editor focuses on the macro vision of the book and will suggest major structural or foundational changes to the first draft. However, a copy editor focuses on the smaller details and specifics of the final manuscript. If necessary, they may perform a minor rewrite to fix any problems with transitions, wordiness, diction, and to ensure the book's style is uniform. Finally, they will check for consistency, factual correctness, and in some instances, potential legal liabilities. A copy editor is essentially the cleanup crew that follows behind your last revisions before the proofreader conducts one last review.

Every book benefits from the expertise of a patient and tedious professional who is skilled at fine-tuning every single aspect of every single sentence and page.

A proofreader is the final set of eyes who reviews the manuscript before it goes to printing. They ensure the pages are perfect: correct spelling, accessible layout, proper punctuation, no typos, error-free grammar. Once your book has been edited, laid out, and designed, proofreading is the last opportunity to correct any issues that might have been missed previously.

A meticulous proofreader will make certain that your book, and you, don't look unprofessional. Beyond hampering your credibility as an author, errors in your book will imply that you're careless. Mistakes like this may seem insignificant, but this can, and often will, cost you readers—and potentially business. Few authors can trust their writing to be technically perfect on its own.

Every book benefits from the expertise of a patient and tedious professional who is skilled at fine-tuning every single aspect of every single sentence and page. The more time spent on a project, the harder it becomes to catch any mistakes, especially when they're as simple as a misplaced comma or a repeated word.

As the author, you will have spent an inordinate amount of time writing and revising your manuscript, and your focus on small details is bound to have lessened. Reward the time spent planning and writing by enlisting a set of trained eyes to ensure that the text is completely free of any technical issues.

The personalized service from a copy editor and proofreader will contribute most to the successful completion of a high-quality book that can boost your brand.

Freelance copy editors and proofreaders are available online. Their fees vary, since their ranges are indicative of their experience and skill level. Be mindful if you hire from online job boards: some sites lack oversight, have slow turnaround, and present untrained practitioners as professionals.

Another inexpensive and oftentimes free alternative is to copy and paste your manuscript into an online SaaS (software as a service) that detects spelling and grammar errors. These platforms use AI to identify mistakes and search for appropriate corrections; some can detect plagiarism and allow users to customize their style, tone, and context-specific language.

There are a few cons: these text editors are not necessarily designed for books, so it can be time-consuming and there is a risk of a security breach. In addition, AI programs lack the human judgment needed for context-specific corrections. Although AI can be programmed to know many grammar rules, they can fail to offer sufficient and effective alternatives to correct sentence structure and paragraph flow. Ultimately, the personalized service from a copy editor and proofreader will contribute most toward your goal: a high-quality, brand-boosting book.

SUMMARY

- ✍ Once your book has been revised, laid out, and designed, copy editing and proofreading are the last opportunities to correct any errors that might have been missed.

- ✍ Errors in your book will imply that you're careless and can, and often will, cost you readers—and potentially business.

- ✍ A copy editor fixes any problems with transitions, wordiness, diction, and ensures the book's style is uniform. They will check for consistency, factual correctness, and in some instances, potential legal liabilities.

- ✍ A proofreader is trained to complete a final review of the manuscript and detect any technical errors that you may be unable to see after spending so much time looking at it.

CHAPTER 14
Formatting Your Manuscript

Professional formatting is integral to the overall quality of your book. The content could be illuminating and well-written, but if the layout is unattractive or ineffective, the audience may misconstrue your book— and thus your brand—as weak and unappealing.

Not hiring a qualified professional to configure the text and any accompanying illustrations can risk projecting that your book is the work of a novice. A poorly-formatted book is an example of bad branding; the core of the work, whether it's your book or business, can be excellent, but communicating that quality effectively requires a polished message.

First-time authors often underestimate the importance of a book's layout. Inferior formatting and visual layouts will affect a book's readability. Some authors look to cut costs by formatting the interior text themselves, though this approach often results in an obviously amateur product.

It may seem simple, but transforming a manuscript into a printed book is not a matter of uploading a file, adjusting margins, and inserting page numbers and chapter headings. There are two aspects to this process: *typesetting* (such as the font, type size, and space between the lines) and *layout* (the margins, columns, and illustrations). In short, typesetting concerns the actual arrangement of the text for print, while the layout, also called the "mise en page" in the publishing industry, refers to the formatting of the pages.

Whether you choose to hire a professional or do the work yourself, ensure that the quality of this step reflects the quality of your brand.

Readers don't notice the typesetting unless it's wrong, at which point, it draws attention to itself and is distracting. Excellent typesetting should not be obvious—it should be the standard. However, designing a book's interior is still laborious because it involves a variety of elements, including:

- ✍ trim size (the height and width of the pages, which vary by book sizes and formats)
- ✍ text boxes or excerpts
- ✍ illustrations, graphics, and photographs
- ✍ page and section breaks
- ✍ font typefaces and sizes (for the body, chapter starts, captions, etc.)

Once these elements are decided, the actual process of setting the text and illustrations on the page begins. Formatting professionals can be found online or through the reverse-search method: review the layouts of independently-published books until you find one you like, then contact the author to ask who did their design work. Note that your options may be limited since some designers only work with established authors, have a backlog of work, or are cost-prohibitive. Keep in mind that layout professionals who charge lower rates will likely produce low-quality results.

Depending on the amount of work involved, your time frame, and any specialized formatting, a reputable professional can cost upwards of four or five figures. They possess highly specialized skills and are paid accordingly. Critics may think that laying out text should be as easy as playing golf. But like golf, there are a hundred details that a professional must learn to perfect and deliver.

When choosing someone to format your book, it's best to:

1. <u>Find someone who's familiar with and understands your readers.</u> Every designer has their own style, and your hire should be proficient in the style that matches your book's market.

2. <u>Review their work.</u> Ask for their portfolio and determine if their designs vary from book to book, and if they have an example of one that fits your genre.

3. <u>Ask questions.</u> Inquire about their process and how they normally work with authors. If they don't readily reply, or you're not satisfied with their answers, keep looking.

If you're willing to take a gamble, you can conduct some research and explore doing the work yourself. But the choices are not abundant. The small selection of available programs that offer layouts require time, intense concentration, and sometimes money. Some downloadable programs convert a word document into a print-ready (PDF) and eBook (EPUB) file, but they can be difficult to navigate and the results can be dubious. Many programs run directly through a webpage, so no downloading is required; however, they aren't very user-friendly and often produce a low-grade layout as well.

A final alternative to hiring a professional is to purchase a license for a desktop publishing and page layout software program. The leading systems provide the tools to create books, magazines, eBooks, and the like. Primarily aimed at production professionals who work for magazines, advertising agencies, newspapers, and commercial printing companies, the technology is somewhat sophisticated.

While the various suites may appear fairly simple to use and can deliver professional-looking results, there are some considerable drawbacks, including your computer needing to meet the minimum technical specifications. Furthermore, some products are only compatible with Mac products.

But as with any other OS-exclusive software, there is a workaround. You can download a program on Windows to essentially run your device like a Mac. However, if you're planning to write and publish several books, then the cost (not including the time required to become proficient) may pay for itself.

Like most of the publishing process, there are several options to completing the formatting and interior layout. Whether you choose to hire a professional or do the work yourself, ensure that the quality of this step reflects the quality of your brand.

SUMMARY

✍ Neglecting to get the text and any accompanying illustrations expertly configured can risk projecting that your book is the work of a novice.

✍ To create the best reading experience for your audience, it's paramount that your book's interior is professional, polished, and engaging.

✍ Layout professionals who charge lower rates will often produce low-quality results.

✍ If a top-tier professional is cost prohibitive, you can explore the DIY option of purchasing a layout software.

CHAPTER 15
Designing the Cover

The cliché is true—*people absolutely judge a book by its cover.* You may have written a book that showcases your brand like none other, but no one will pick it up if it doesn't catch their attention. That's why the cover design can make or break your book's success.

It's rare for a book to succeed in spite of a bad cover. Oftentimes, an author may not know what constitutes a good book cover. Cover design is not their expertise—writing about their industry is. If left to their own devices, most authors would design a book cover that would not do their book—and, by extension, their brand—any justice.

The number one goal for a book cover is to evoke interest. Once this is accomplished, the person browsing will glance at the title, catch a glimpse of your brand, maybe flip it over to scan the key phrases and, if presented properly, get an understanding of your subject. All of this occurs within a few seconds.

Your cover doesn't have to be spectacular in color, unique in style, or flashy in its title. It just needs to quickly engage the reader and prompt them to read the few key pieces of information presented:

- ✍ What topic the book explores and who the intended audience is.

- ✍ What a reader can learn from the book.

- ✍ Why a reader should want to read *this* book written by *this* person.

Since you're publishing a book to build your brand, you'll want to match the color scheme to your website and include your company logo or tagline in the cover design.

A good cover will reflect and reinforce all of the time and work you've put into the content; if the outside of the package is unappealing, the contents are often (unfairly) dismissed as such too. So if you want to make your book appear to be worth reading, the cover needs to be captivating. This happens by employing the right mix of colors, fonts, text, size, format, images, and other visual elements that all combine to form the overall cover design. It needs to have a "know when you see it" quality.

A cover offers valuable clues to potential readers about what they may find inside a book. It can also give prospective customers a brief introduction into your business. Since you're publishing a book to build your brand, you'll want to match the color scheme to your website and include your company logo or tagline in the cover design.

There are a variety of free online platforms and programs that can be used to design a cover. If you decide to distribute your book via Kindle Direct Publishing, there is an option to create a cover during the manuscript uploading process. KDP's Cover Creator provides complimentary stock photos and basic templates for authors publishing on their platform. However, this method will certainly lack the high-quality appearance of professional work, and so your book's marketability may suffer.

If you're seeking a specific style, you can perform the aforementioned Amazon search for similar books and contact the author for information regarding their cover designer. Another option is to purchase any one of a variety of software programs that are used for image editing and creating high-quality graphics. If you are willing to spend a considerable amount of time to become proficient, you might be able to create a credible cover that effectively communicates your brand message. However, with so many features to learn, these programs may be too complicated for many users to successfully navigate.

To save yourself from the time and stress that a personal endeavor would most likely entail, you should invest in a professional graphic designer. A mediocre cover with an acceptable brand message could take you a month's worth of time and headaches, whereas an experienced designer could generate several professional covers in a few weeks.

By investigating freelance sites, an outside hire does not necessarily have to be expensive. There are countless low-cost designers who still produce high-quality results, so long as you take the time to weed through the options. Reputable designers will often post their credentials and portfolios to prove their abilities, and many sites even provide reviews from past clients. Although experienced designers may have higher fees, the finished product is usually worth the added expense.

A final option for finding talent is an online platform that connects authors directly to artists, as well as provides an avenue to conduct a design contest. Project specifications are provided along with design preferences, any specific wording or themes, and any necessary visual elements to include. Then within a set time frame, any interested artists submit a range of designs. The author gives feedback on the designs they like until a finalist is chosen.

Since every format has different dimensions and file requirements, the design will need to be rendered in the proper size and specifications for every format the book will be published in, including at least the paperback and eBook versions, and possibly the hardback and audiobook as well.

A book's dimensions, known within the industry as its "trim size," are typically determined by the genre it falls under. There is a range of commonly accepted sizes within each classification. The exceptions are mass market paperbacks and comic books, which generally conform to an industry-wide standard.

The following are the common standards for popular genres:

- ✍ Mass market paperbacks: 4.25" x 6.87"

- ✍ Comic books: 6.625" x 10.25"

- ✍ Fiction and general nonfiction paperbacks range from 5" x 8" to 6" x 9"

- ✍ Novellas: 5" x 8"

- ✍ Hardbacks: 6" x 9"

- ✍ Textbooks, which frequently include illustrations and diagrams, range from 6" x 9" to 8.5" x 11"

Regardless of your book's genre, the cover and internal designs can either add quality to the final product, or diminish the perception of your content. DIY cover designs are an option, though many authors hire a professional to design their book's cover. The cover design is projecting a message to potential readers before they've even glimpsed the book's content, so make sure it's an accurate representation of your brand and the book.

SUMMARY

- The number one goal for a book cover is to catch the reader's attention (in a positive way).

- The cover can give potential customers a glimpse of your business.

- Utilizing a professional artist will be a worthwhile investment to get the best results and save you valuable time and energy.

- The cover design will need to be rendered in the proper size and specifications for every format that the book will be published in.

CHAPTER 16
Writing the Book Description

A front cover is critical. Just like a brand's logo, it's what initially grabs attention. But once a potential reader picks up the book or clicks on the title, what do they do next? They flip it over or scroll down the screen. Why? To read the description on the back cover, which tells them what the book is about and makes a pitch for them to read it.

An attractive front cover is what draws a potential reader in, but the description on the back cover is what seals the deal. A well-written and effective description can ultimately win over anyone on the fence. Showcasing what defines your brand, it's the "sales pitch," and thus needs to be a succinct and polished message. It should give the reader just enough details to understand what the book is about and expressly state what it can do for them.

When someone is considering a book to read, their first question is generally, "What can I get out of it?" For nonfiction, this usually means what they'll learn and how they can use this information to improve their lives. This is why your book's description can't simply allude to what's in it for them; you need to tell them outright. How they will benefit from reading your book is the entire selling point—you must make this loud and clear.

If your book addresses an issue that needs to be solved, the problem statement can be the hook that catches the attention of potential readers. You can reel them in by listing a few key points that the book will discuss, while not providing the specific resolution.

The better your book description, the better your chances are for gaining visibility and your brand remaining on the minds of prospective readers.

Like an elevator speech, an effective description says much, but in as few words as needed. It grabs the reader's attention, provides the essence of the book, hints at the content inside, and compels someone to want to learn more. It doesn't over-explain and give the whole book away, overtly stroke the author's ego, promise more than it can deliver, or bore the reader.

This may seem like a lot to accomplish in only a few hundred words, but it won't be difficult if you consider the potential reader's perspective and answer these questions:

- ✍ What main point will get their attention?

- ✍ What types of information will they most want?

- ✍ What distinguishes you as an authority whom they should listen to?

- ✍ What stories will you tell?

- ✍ What is your unique insight?

The back cover description from Scott's first book is an effective example:

As someone in technology, you have an incredibly specialized expertise that companies desperately need. So, why are you at the mercy of whatever a recruiter or HR feels like paying you?

You don't know how to sell your labor at the best price, and you're suffering for it. The difference between struggling on an unfair rate and making thousands of extra dollars a year is all in negotiation, the critical lesson that you've never been taught.

Until now.

It's time to take the power back. You can and should be able to make a comfortable living off of your skillset, and I'm going to use my 20+ years experience in the industry to show you how to do just that. This book exposes all of the recruiter's dirty little tricks, the racket going on behind salary and benefits, and ultimately teaches you to negotiate for the best rate that you can really get.

There are several reasons why this description works. The title already appeals to a very specific audience (IT professionals), so the first paragraph grabs their attention by describing the common problem within its audience (being taken advantage of by technical recruiters). The next paragraph further describes this problem, and the final paragraph explains what this book will teach them (how to negotiate), and how it will benefit them (through higher pay). The diction and direct structure reinforce the sustained tone and style within the book, and Scott's credentials are referenced (many years of experience in the industry). Ideally, this book description acts as a bundled sales pitch that appeals to a prospective reader, their problem, and why they should read the book.

There's no definitive formula for writing a great description; the key is to get the reader so engrossed in the book's concept that it leaves them wanting more. The better your book description, the better your chances are for gaining visibility and your brand remaining on their mind. The description needs to help potential buyers easily find and understand your book, so consider what key terms, industries, products, or services someone might search for when looking for a book like yours, and then enhance your description based on those findings.

Your editor and beta readers, as well as those in your target audience, can act as a sounding board for the book description. They should be able to provide an objective review and give honest feedback on how to improve it.

An effective book description isn't a task you can complete in a rush. Carefully crafted descriptions need to offer a balance of information with a curiosity to learn more. Though it's a puzzle to piece together, a compelling book description can turn potential readers into committed buyers who engage with your brand.

SUMMARY

- An attractive front cover is what draws a potential reader in, but the description on the back cover is what seals the deal.

- A good book description grabs the reader's attention, provides the essence of the book, hints at the content inside, and compels someone to want to learn more.

- The description's key terms need to help potential buyers easily find and understand your book.

CHAPTER 17

Composing Your Author Biography

The back cover gives a preview of the book's contents, but it also shows a snapshot of you and your brand. Your author bio is just as important as the description. The objective is clear: in a concise and alluring paragraph (no more than 300 words), introduce yourself to potential readers and explain your credentials as an authority on your book's subject.

Your bio needs to be well-written because more people will ultimately read it than your book's content. It takes hours to read your book, but it only takes a minute to read an author's bio and make a snap decision to determine if you're worth the reader's time. Furthermore, your personal summary may influence whether someone wants to do business with you, regardless of whether they even open your book.

Your biography can highlight your credibility, detail your qualifications, and legitimize what you've written. It's crucial because although not everyone necessarily reads an author's bio, those who do often use it as the deciding factor for whether they'll trust what you've written. A bio that doesn't affirm your authority might do more harm than you think, while a well-written one can improve sales, strengthen your reputation, boost marketing, and propel your social media presence.

People are more comfortable conducting business with people they know, and by including a professional photograph, you can build an affinity to you and your brand.

Any personal information, beyond mentioning your family or where you live, should only be included if it distinguishes your expertise and contributes to making your brand distinct. Any irrelevant accomplishments should be excluded as well as personal information that could risk crossing the line of professionalism. Approach your bio as an opportunity to connect with your prospective readers and cultivate a sense of relationship.

Standard biography guidelines:

- Write in the third-person.

- Begin with one simple, interesting sentence. (Be careful with using a quip. It may not go over well with every reader.)

- Briefly describe yourself and your qualifications as if you're meeting a prospective client for the first time, but don't be too flattering.

- Add two or three relevant achievements or credentials.

- ✎ If applicable, share your title, company name, and website.
- ✎ Use only a headshot, taken by a professional.

If you're unsure of what to write, you can refer to author biographies in books similar to yours. By reading a few, you will develop an understanding of how to write your own.

It's the industry standard for an author's picture to accompany their biography. Although you might be camera shy or believe a photo is unnecessary, including one can indirectly build rapport and even trust.

People are more comfortable conducting business with people they know, and by including a professional photograph, you can build an affinity to you and your brand. The physiological reasoning for including a photo is that humans are visual creatures. We rely on physical characteristics and facial expressions to make judgments of each other, including perceived social status, level of intelligence, and even economic standing. We utilize our sight to help sense attraction, determine if we would like to associate with someone, and judge if they appear trustworthy. Although somewhat cerebral, this premise furthers the rationale of why to include your photograph on your book's back cover.

The photo needs to look sharp, be indicative of your personality, convey the message you want to promote, and match the "tone" of the voice you present within the book. With this in mind, there are several attributes to avoid, including:

- Don't wear anything overly bright, patterned, ill-fitting, or otherwise distracting. You want what you wear to be fashionable, but otherwise inconsequential.

- Don't use a tight close-up picture or one taken from an odd angle, such as below the waist.

- Don't choose a distracting background. Use a neutral one or have it align with the book's subject (at your desk, in front of your workplace, with a group of clients, or even with your logo superimposed), but don't take the focus away from you. If there are people in the background, make sure they can't be easily identified.

- Don't use any filters since most digital alterations (beyond fixing red eyes and blurring the errant blemish) are obvious and could lose you some trust with your readers.

To avoid an amateur, unpolished product, it's important to hire a professional photographer. As you build your author brand, you'll likely use the same photo for other marketing purposes, such as blog posts and press kits, as well as on your Amazon author page. It can be among the most important marketing messages you'll craft, so take care to choose your photo wisely and support it with a convincing author bio.

SUMMARY

- The purpose of an author biography is to tell prospective readers about yourself and establish your credibility.

- A well-written biography can improve sales, strengthen your reputation, boost marketing, and propel your social media presence.

- Including your photograph will build trust and a connection between you and your readers.

- The same author photo will be used for marketing purposes such as blog posts and press kits, as well as on your Amazon author page.

CHAPTER 18
Understanding ISBN, Keywords, and Categories

If you've ever flipped to the back page of a book, you may have noticed a barcode and a series of numbers and letters printed on the bottom. The 13-digit code is the International Standard Book Number, or the ISBN. An ISBN allows someone to search all of the details of your book, connects it to multiple databases, and increases its overall visibility. If you want to cement your book's legitimacy, then you need to obtain an ISBN.

An ISBN is one of the biggest differentiators between an "amateur" self-published book, and a "professional" independently-published one. If your book does not have an ISBN, then the distribution platform that you publish your book on will simply assign a barcode and code used only for its in-network identification. For example, KDP will assign what they call an ASIN, or an Amazon Standard Identification Number. These codes stand out and are the most evident indicator that a book was not professionally published.

Including an ISBN will make it nearly impossible for the average reader to know whether or not you published your book independently. An ISBN is what takes your book from a personal project to a legitimate product that can be classified, accessed, and ordered based on its internationally recognized identifier.

An ISBN will connect your book to multiple databases. This increases the likelihood of it being discovered by additional book shoppers, which in turn may increase sales. If the intent is to have brick-and-mortar stores carry your book, an ISBN is required since no bookstore will carry a book without one. Even if online distribution is the sole focus, an ISBN offers tremendous benefits.

To classify the book into its appropriate categories, it's best to start by determining its leading keywords. They should be as identical as possible to those used to describe your brand.

The easiest way to procure an ISBN is through Bowker Identifier Services. Their website conducts the ISBN-assignment application process to register either as an individual, publishing organization, LLC, or any other type of entity. You can purchase a single ISBN or multiple ones at a discount of ten for $295. Since each book format requires a separate ISBN, you may need to purchase up to four ISBNs for each publication (paperback, audiobook, digital, and hardcover). And since they never expire, you can use any leftover ISBNs for future books.

As the official ISBN agency for publishers operating out of the United States and its territories, Bowker will collect a variety of the book's details, such as the author, description, and publication date. In addition, you'll need to define three elements: the keywords, categories, and pricing.

To classify the book into its appropriate categories, it's best to start by determining its leading keywords. They should be as identical as possible to those used to describe your brand, especially since the words and phrases used to characterize your book determine the book's general placement and its two or three major labels.

The keywords used to describe a book are similar to Search Engine Optimization (SEO) keywords. In the same regard, it's sensible to choose the words and phrases that direct browsing customers to your book. The best ones will be niche and very specific. For instance, if you've written a book detailing the best methods of orchestrating hostile takeovers, "hostile" and "takeovers" are a good start. But "best hostile takeover methods" will be more effective terms to steer possible readers to your book.

As you continue to classify your book into its appropriate categories, you may think that grouping a number of frequently searched words and phrases will garner more attention. However, this practice is unlikely to attract any potential readers if those keywords aren't related to your book. Furthermore, there's even a risk of not reaching those readers who *want* to find your book. It's a matter of the descriptive quality of the words versus the quantity. And, there's the added jeopardy of getting flagged for spam by misusing keywords. Therefore, it's crucial to choose the descriptors that best match your book.

It can be challenging to pinpoint the allotted keywords that fit your book *and* are most strategic for SEO. The best way to accomplish this is by listing every word that describes your book and then narrowing it down to the best terms and phrases that fit. The first part of this culling process is to simply cross out or delete the terms least related to your book. Following this, input the remaining keywords to any of the keyword research tools available online to determine their individual search frequencies.[1] Then, list and rank the respective numbers for each word to produce the final ranking.

By knowing the micro (keywords), you'll be able to determine the macro (categories). Placing your book in the proper categories is critical to reaching someone who is browsing. To identify the proper categories, you must perform research over how the book's subject fits into the different categories and subcategories available. Comparable to keywords, the best categories are strategically chosen but still *specific* to your book and its contents. For instance, a book on Elon Musk might fall under "biographies" or "technology," but depending on the book's specific subject matter, these may not necessarily be the proper classifications.

---

1   One of the most common is Keywords Explorer, available on Ahrefs. Any one of the assorted online tools will be able to indicate how often a word or phrase is searched.

There's a sweet spot between where your book can be found and where it can achieve its best ranking. Amazon ranks books based on sales and reviews for both their entire inventory and for each category.

To determine which categories someone might search to find a book like yours, the process is the same as choosing keywords. The chosen categories should strike a balance between those that best fit your book and those that are most conducive to achieving the highest ranking possible. This involves identifying categories with less competition but are still where a potential reader may search. Everything on your list should fit and be "rankable."

To start, take the categories you have listed and find the number one book in each. In the book's product details, you'll be able to see their best seller rank. The first number is the book's rank in the entire Amazon store for all of its books. Once you have the number for each category, access a "best seller calculator" available online. There's one for the Kindle and one for physical books, so make sure that the calculator and numbers you're using correlate to the proper market.

The calculators will indicate approximately how many books any particular title needs to sell each day in order to maintain its overall rank in the Amazon store. The lower its calculated daily sales are, the less competitive the category is. These low-competition categories that fit your book are the ones you want to choose.

There's a sweet spot between where your book can be found and where it can achieve its best ranking. Amazon ranks books based on sales and reviews for both their entire inventory and each category. Their algorithm computes this data and adjusts rankings. The higher your book ranks, the more visible it becomes to potential readers. When a book hits the top spot in either the store or its category, it earns the coveted "Best Seller" banner. This elevates your book's prominence and makes you a "best-selling author."

But a bestseller isn't always a best-selling book. Some independent authors have learned to manipulate the system by setting their book in the most niche, least competitive category in order to receive that status. (There are even marketing agencies that charge outrageous fees to accomplish this.) While this maneuver can technically label you as a "best-selling author," it will end up severely hampering your potential for readers and risk tarnishing your brand. By placing your book in the most niche category possible, prospective readers won't be able to find it. Unless you'd rather receive imagined prestige over more readers, it's best to place your book where potential readers will search.

The last decision to make when registering for an ISBN is the price for each book format. Since distinguishing yourself as an expert, building your brand, and creating opportunities are probably your main goal—as opposed to making a profit through book sales—you may reason that it would be sensible to set the pricing low. However, you should actually price it higher than what you may think. Too low of a cost, and potential readers will wonder what is "wrong" with your book that makes it so cheap.

Setting your book's appropriate price is a matter of reviewing the common price point for books of similar length in its categories. But when completing the information on the ISBN form, it's prudent to increase the estimated figure by $5-$10. It may seem counter-intuitive, but this is a common practice within retail sales. Consider how Kohl's clothing store is always having a mark-down sale; the prices afterward seem like a deal too good to pass up. By listing a book's price higher on the ISBN and offering it for lower on Amazon, buyers often get the sense that they're getting a discount.

This is bolstered by Amazon sometimes highlighting an item's savings not only in dollars and cents, but also by a percentage. Because shoppers are conditioned to think that Amazon always offers the lowest online prices, they won't shop on other sites. Your book becomes a bargain without damaging the perception of its quality.

Investing in an ISBN and selecting the appropriate keywords, categories, and price for your book are crucial steps for successful marketing. It's not enough to write the book and ensure its quality; you have to strategically place the book where potential readers can find it. These keywords and categories techniques can help direct traffic to your sales pitch, where the book description, ISBN credibility, and price will seal the deal.

SUMMARY

✎ Your book should have an ISBN, or International Standard Book Number, which is a 13-digit numerical code to link it to databases and increase its visibility.

 📖 Without an ISBN, your book will be given an internal number and barcode by your publishing platform, which can be an indicator of a self-published book.

 📖 Bowker Identifier Services is the official ISBN Agency for publishers physically located in the United States and its territories.

✎ A book's publication date, description, keywords, categories, and price need to be determined at this point.

✎ It can be challenging to pinpoint the few allotted keywords that both fit your book and are most strategic for SEO.

✎ Placing your book in its proper categories requires performing research to understand how its subject correlates into different categories and subcategories, and which ones are best for achieving a high ranking.

- Amazon ranks books based on sales and reviews for both their entire inventory and for each category.

- By listing its price higher on the ISBN and offering it lower on Amazon, buyers often get the sense that they're getting a discount.

PART V

PUBLISHING

CHAPTER 19

Disrupting Traditional Publishing

Like many institutions, the publishing industry is constantly evolving and adapting to stay relevant. There was a time when many successful authors, the backbone of the business, could earn a living solely from their book's royalties. But for most, those earnings were greatly diminished with the advent of the Internet.

Disruption in the publishing industry has happened in the same way that video stores were replaced with streaming services, small-town shops with Walmarts, and bank tellers with electronic banking. The former has a diminishing degree of presence, while the latter will continue to grow and overtake what was once the status quo. In short, the publishing industry is at a crossroads.

With so many digital distractions, most people don't read printed books (as well as magazines and newspapers) during their downtime anymore. The market is *tough*, to say the least, and traditional publishing houses know this.

One consequence of this is that few publishers take risks on first-time authors. Publishers need a guarantee that an unknown writer's book will be profitable, or else they won't take the chance. Thus, if you're not a promising presidential candidate, internationally known businessman with a cutting-edge product, a prominent CEO who just announced their retirement, or have a timely manuscript that hits the current news cycle at the right time, there's little chance they'll consider working with you.

Through tireless efforts, there's a chance that you and your manuscript could land a contract with a traditional publishing company. The following is a brief synopsis of the process.

First, you start by sending a query letter to various literary agents. Most publishing houses won't accept an unsolicited manuscript, meaning one without agent representation. If you're lucky, you will receive a few replies with a request for some chapter samples or even a full read of the book. Finding a literary agent to represent you is often a long and tedious process filled with rejection letters and radio silence, regardless of your book's quality.

If you are able to sign with an agent, they might pitch you to a publisher who could decide to purchase the rights to your book. If a publisher owns the rights to your book, they are able to make changes as they see fit, which can include modifying the content and organization. They will select the title, choose covers and designs you might find distasteful, and place the burden of promotional work on you. You might receive a four-figure advance and if your book sales earn this back, you earn royalties. Usually, this percentage is less than a quarter of net sales and in most cases, hardback books earn 10% while paperbacks earn 7.5% ("Buying Choices").

A traditional publisher will oversee a wide variety of details and assume the financial risk of not only printing thousands of copies of your book, but also the associated distribution and marketing expenses. In addition, they will also coordinate the production of the digital and audio formats, and absorb the upfront costs.

Factoring in the hours spent writing and revising your manuscript, as well as opportunities missed while writing, it's possible that you would not earn enough to make the endeavor worthwhile. But this scenario reflects publishing a book to make money, not to create business opportunities. Next, we'll talk about the "new path": independent publishing.

SUMMARY

✍ The traditional publishing industry has changed in many ways and is experiencing disruption.

✍ Few publishers take risks on first-time authors due to the competition of the market.

✍ While a traditional publisher will pay an advance and handle all publishing details, they take creative control, delegate marketing responsibilities to the author, and take the vast majority of royalties.

CHAPTER 20
Introducing Independent Publishing

An independently published book is an entrepreneurial endeavor. To clarify, independent publishing is not the same as self-publishing, nor is it a vanity project.

Self-publishing is when an author completes or pays for their own editing, formatting, cover design, and even printing. The quality of the product varies depending on the author's skill, available time, and allocated budget. Vanity publishing is a similar process where the author pays someone to turn a manuscript—regardless of quality—into a book without doing any editing, designing, or marketing. In contrast to other publishing methods, vanity publishers frequently intend to profit off of authors' lack of publishing knowledge without producing high quality books for readers.

The definition of independent publishing is simple: *it's a publishing process where an author remains autonomous and makes their own decisions.* They either have the skillset to fulfill each step, or they choose to employ professionals to complete the process for them. Generally, these individuals publish their book for the opportunity—not necessarily for the royalties—to tell their story, share their expertise, leave a legacy, or distinguish their brand.

With the increasing popularity of eBooks and Print-on-Demand (POD) distributors, it's easier than ever to have your book published and into the hands of readers.

Independent publishing has a long history rooted in responding against "the system." Independent publishing in America can trace its roots back to the early colonists, such as Benjamin Franklin, who published the *Pennsylvania Gazette* as well as numerous books (Wood). To a certain extent, American independence itself can be linked to independent publishing after Thomas Paine Paine published "Common Sense," a pamphlet which criticized British rule over the colonists and boldly pushed for independence ("The American Revolution"). An independently published book doesn't have to start a literal revolution, but it should showcase what makes your brand or experience remarkable.

Being an independent publisher doesn't mean you can't succeed in traditional publishing. It's not a "second choice" avenue for authors, but one with measurable benefits and equal prestige. Many talented authors have independently published their books. Whether they couldn't find a publisher or didn't like the contract offer, some of these authors went on to achieve tremendous success.

For many other authors, independent publishing is the solution to all of the problems inherent to traditional publishing. And with the increasing popularity of eBooks and Print-on-Demand (POD) distributors, it's easier than ever to have your book published and into the hands of readers.

Choosing the independent alternative means you retain complete creative control of your book from cover to cover. As previously explained, you may have to find and pay for editing, cover design, proofreading, and layout services, but you'll manage the entire process and call all of the shots. You have the final say on your book and you're not held inferior to anyone else. For many other authors, autonomy is more than worth the upfront expense.

Of course, you won't receive an advance with independent publishing, but there's also no advance that your book sales need to earn back. You start collecting royalties on the very first sale, which typically range anywhere from 30%-70%. That's significantly more than any traditional publisher would ever offer.

Traditional publishers usually require their authors to perform an array of marketing and advertising duties without paying them any extra advance or royalties in return. In contrast, as an independent author, you'll realize a direct payoff for your work since you alone will earn the additional profits from your efforts.

While there are many different distribution platforms available for independent publishing, there's one primary site to consider. Unequivocally, Amazon's Kindle Direct Publishing (KDP) platform is the best option available. Because of Amazon's dominance in just about every imageable market, they can reach more customers than all of their competitors combined.

You can place your book on other platforms, but KDP is the premier choice.

If you choose to publish exclusively on KDP, then you have the option to enroll your book in a feature called "KDP Unlimited." It allows readers to access any books enrolled in the program for a monthly subscription fee rather than paying for each book individually. This is a great deal for someone who reads a lot, and it can be profitable for you as well.

Authors receive a monthly disbursement based on how much all Kindle Unlimited readers paid in subscription fees and the number of Kindle Edition Normalized Pages (KENP) subscribers read of their books.

Some have argued that paying authors by the number of pages read is unfair to those who have enrolled their graphic novels, children's books, and other works that typically have a lower overall page count. Nonetheless, Kindle Unlimited is an extra option that can generate more readers, and in turn, more revenue. It's especially well-suited for those who aren't planning to publish their book on other platforms, have lengthier books, or simply want to reach as many readers as possible.

Independent publishing through platforms like KDP allows you to maintain creative control over your book, and by extension, your brand's message. If you're looking to keep a hold of the reins and reap the full benefits of your book, independent publishing is your best option.

SUMMARY

- The definition of independent publishing is a publishing process that allows an author to remain autonomous and make their own decisions.

- Independent publishing is a great option for entrepreneurs and those who want to retain creative control of their book.

- As an independent author, you will have to manage the production details, pay upfront associated costs, and will not receive an advance, but you will earn higher royalties.

- With the increasing popularity of eBooks and Print-on-Demand (POD) distributors, it's easier than ever to have your book published and into the hands of readers.

- KDP, or Kindle Direct Publishing, is the best platform available on the market for independent publishing.

  - Your book can be available on Kindle and the Amazon marketplace through their Print-on-Demand service.

- Enrolling your book in Kindle Unlimited gives you an additional opportunity to reach readers.

CHAPTER 21
Creating an eBook

Given the prevalence of eBooks, many people now choose to read exclusively in a digital format. The convenience of using one lightweight device to read and access thousands of books has undeniable appeal.

While a printed book needs to be ordered and delivered or purchased from a store (with time and effort involved for each), an eBook can be in a reader's hands almost instantaneously. Authors can always change content, publish new editions, or add the up-to-date information without needing to print and distribute new versions, which saves time, money, and resources. An eBook version includes features that decrease eye strain, such as changing the size of the fonts as well as changing the device's brightness. These qualities combined make a book's digital version appeal to the largest possible audience.

Some authors may have reservations about creating a digital version of their book, driven by their ego and a misguided sense of legitimacy. They may rationalize that if their manuscript is not printed in ink and on paper, then it's not a "real" book. Thus, one of the biggest mistakes a first-time author can make is to reject the potential of a digital-access audience because of their own opinions on what a "real book" is. By limiting the availability to only printed copies, authors miss out on a large portion of potential readers.

The purpose of publishing a book to build your brand is to create business opportunities by becoming a recognized expert in your field.

An eBook is undeniably a "real" book. All of the most famous and widely-read books—*The 7 Habits of Highly Effective People*, *Harry Potter*, *The Essays of Warren Buffett*, *War and Peace*, *The South Beach Diet*, everything—are available in print *and* digital formats. In fact, most traditionally published books are available in both versions. Following this standard practice and offering both versions will contribute to your book being recognized as legitimate work.

Releasing a book in its digital format first can be advantageous to establishing a higher ranking in its respective categories. Since eBook rankings are typically easier to achieve than paperback, this can greatly increase a book's chances of earning a "Best-Seller" banner at the top of its Amazon page.

Publishing an eBook through Amazon's Kindle Direct Program simply requires supplying information and uploading the book's cover and specialized EPUB text layout file. If you've registered the book's ISBN, then most of the work will have already been completed for you. Most of the required information, including categories and keywords, can be copied and pasted from the ISBN. Be sure to check that you're providing the correct ISBN for your eBook, since each ISBN is specific to each book format.

It's imperative that the cover be correctly rendered, especially since an eBook doesn't include the back cover and accompanying information that a paperback does. Instead, the book description and author bio will be available directly on the sales page.

Another main difference between the eBook and paperback formats is that an eBook is generally priced lower than a paperback, since it requires no physical materials to produce. eBook sales earn a 70% royalty on Amazon if it's priced between $2.99 and $9.99 in most markets. For books priced less than $2.99 or more than $9.99, the percentage drops to 35%, which is still much higher than the royalties earned through a traditional publishing agreement. However, since an eBook price can be changed frequently, it's best to experiment with different price points.

Although it may seem counterintuitive, setting your book's price has little to do with maximizing its profits, and a lower price does not necessarily attract more readers. The purpose of publishing a book to build your brand is to create business opportunities by becoming a recognized expert in your field. Pricing your book too low can actually limit this success. Potential readers will gauge the potential quality of your book by what you provide (title, cover, description, first few pages), how others responded to it (reviews and rank), *and* the price you set. While an unreasonably high price could deter many readers, an exceptionally low one will likely make them suspicious about the book's quality.

A reasonably priced book should be commensurate with books in its categories. The eBook version of a book offers more accessibility when compared to the paperback version, so ensure your eBook price is reasonable with respect to the eBook versions of similar subjects.

SUMMARY

- The eBook format is the predominant preference of most readers.

- An eBook can be published through KDP by supplying the information from its ISBN and uploading the correct cover version and EPUB text layout.

- An eBook is generally priced lower than a paperback and will earn a 70% royalty of its sales on Amazon if it's priced between $2.99 and $9.99.

- Pricing your book too low can lead people to think that it is poorly written and not worth buying.

CHAPTER 22
Producing a Paperback

There is a sense of magic when holding a physical copy of the book you wrote. It may be the greatest tangible affirmation of all of your hard work. Seeing your words printed on paper is a thrill, but publishing your manuscript as a paperback serves more than just your ego.

Your prospective clients, peers, and even the media may value and trust you more once you're a published author. While many in your audience may prefer eBooks, there are still readers who are devoted to buying and reading physical copies. While an eBook will reach a lot of readers, both formats can reach almost all of them.

By printing books only when they are ordered, Amazon can offer the paperback option to all authors.

Printing and distributing a paperback is no longer the difficult and tedious process that it once was. Amazon's Print-On-Demand (POD) service empowers all authors to create physical copies of their book without the prohibitive upfront costs that initially made print publishing largely unobtainable for independent authors.

Instead of subscribing to the traditional publisher's practice of mass printing a set number of copies with the hope that they'll sell enough to cover the upfront cost, POD individually prints and ships copies as they are purchased. By printing books only when they are ordered, Amazon can offer the paperback option to all authors.

Arranging to have a paperback printed and distributed via Amazon is just as quick and easy as setting up an eBook. The same information that was submitted for the ISBN and eBook can be used again, taking care to make any necessary changes, such as ensuring that the ISBN, cover, text file, and price are all specific to the paperback version.

Pricing is the most notable difference between the eBook and paperback formats. In almost all geographic markets, a paperback is generally entitled to 60% of royalties, no matter the set price. However, the net royalty is determined only after the cost of production. The KDP printing costs can be determined in three different ways: generating a figure through their calculator after uploading your files, utilizing their pricing tables, or downloading an Excel spreadsheet print cost formulator.

Since a paperback requires material and labor to produce and deliver, Amazon calculates this cost based on the book's length, specified dimensions, type of paper, color, weight, and whether the cover is a gloss or matte finish. (For the cost of production, Amazon offers the option to order a beta copy to review prior to making it available for sale.) The minimum price that can be set for a paperback is based on Amazon's calculated cost of production. Once that is set, Amazon will indicate the royalty to be earned per sale.

As with an eBook, the most important action to take for determining a price is to review comparative books within its category. Most self-published books, especially from first-time authors, are priced lower than traditionally published books. Generally, paperbacks are priced between $9.99 and $19.99, depending on length and subject matter, and the price can be periodically changed as well. Those priced under $6 are usually an indicator that they are self-published. Select a price that reflects your expertise and hard work, but one that is still reasonable for readers to pay.

Offering both the eBook and paperback formats will enable you to reach most of the market, but not quite all of it. Next, we'll talk about those who *listen* to books and how you can capture them with an audiobook format.

SUMMARY

- Offering a paperback can set you apart and allow you to capitalize on your image as a published author.

- KDP offers a POD, or Print-On-Demand, service to publish a paperback format of your book.

- Royalties are generally set at 60% after the cost of production is factored in.

- Production costs include the book's length, specified dimensions, type of paper, color, weight, and whether the cover is a gloss or matte finish.

- Generally, paperbacks are priced between $9.99 and $19.99, depending on length and subject matter.

CHAPTER 23
Recording an Audiobook

Audiobook listeners are a long-established and growing segment of the book market. Some of your audience members may not prefer or have the time to read your book, but still may be interested in listening about you and your brand. Thus, recording an audiobook is essential for your book to reach as many people as possible.

Audiobooks are capturing an even larger share of the reading market as more listening options become available. The adage "listening to a book on tape" applies less often as people swap CDs and tapes for apps that offer streaming services. While many people are too busy to keep their eyes on a page or screen, they can integrate an audiobook into their daily commute or play a book as they exercise, which no other format can offer.

The biggest challenge is hiring a professional narrator to record the reading of the manuscript. Nothing is more critical to your audiobook's success than selecting a voice to articulate your brand.

Since Amazon acquired Audible, it's now just as easy to upload an audiobook as an eBook and paperback. An account on the Audiobook Creation Exchange (ACX) links directly to your KDP account, which makes it easier to upload your book formats. Similar to KDP, the ACX website will take you through the entire process. While royalties for an audiobook are slightly lower, authors still earn 40% royalties on Audible, Amazon, and iTunes.

While audiobook production is more involved and time-consuming than other formats, the biggest challenge is hiring a professional narrator to record the reading of the manuscript. Nothing is more critical to your audiobook's success than selecting a voice to articulate your brand.

There is no shortage of talent available on ACX, which provides the framework to post a call for "producers" to audition. A description of the book, specifications of the exact type of voice desired, and a short sample of the manuscript are available for those interested in auditioning. Narrators then provide audio samples to be considered for the role.

The ideal voice is not necessarily a better, more professional version of your own. Rather, it's important to consider the book's target audience and the type of voice that would best suit the tone of the book. Since it's most likely written in the first person, it's best to choose a narrator who is the same gender as you and can mimic your personal brand. This entails replicating your manner of speaking, such as the pitch you use to express industry jargon, your inflection, and even your accent. Having similarities between your chosen narrator and your own voice will help establish you as the voice of authority without creating a disjointed connection between your words and story, and the audiobook's narrator.

Once the narrator is chosen, an offer is made to contract their services. The agreement will specify the time frame as well as a proposed split of the royalties, or an offer for a set hourly rate, which will interest narrators who are of higher quality. After approving the completed recording, ACX will "greenlight" the audiobook, which will then be available for purchase. The ACX review process can take up to six weeks, so it's best to start production as soon as the eBook is published.

SUMMARY

- A growing number of readers prefer the audio format due to the convenience of listening to books while doing other activities.

- Since Amazon has acquired Audible, it's now just as easy to upload your narrated book as it is to upload an eBook and paperback. The process is as simple as an account on the Audiobook Creation Exchange (ACX) and choosing your narrator.

- Nothing is more critical to your audiobook's success than selecting a voice to articulate your brand.

- Since the ACX review process can take up to six weeks, it's best to start production as soon as the eBook is published.

CHAPTER 24

Releasing a Hardcover

Traditional publishers often release a new title as a hardcover to create prestige, show their support of the author, and validate the (anticipated) value of their investment. Once the book reaches its preliminary sales goals, the standard is to then release the paperback version at a lower price to attract readers who may not have wanted to pay the hardback cost. Or, if the book flops, the publisher will cut their losses by discounting it and not release the paperback at all.

The durability, shelf appeal, and stature associated with hardcover books are features many readers are willing to pay for, and certainly libraries prefer to stock them because they stand up better to repeated use. But for the independent author, publishing a hardcover is often much more trouble than it's worth.

Due to material costs and the time it takes to produce and distribute them, hardcover books are usually priced higher than the paperback versions. But if the higher costs can be justified, such as to garner prestige, announce a new product, recognize an achievement, commemorate a special date, provide to prospective clients, or even to award as a prize, it may be worthwhile to print the more expensive format.

Offering your readers a hardback may also help legitimize your book and further contribute to building your brand. It certainly helps project your sense of authority, and your distinctions can be highlighted in a dust jacket.

The process to produce a hardcover is much more complicated than any other format. Although KDP offers a beta hardcover POD service, their process can be cumbersome and time-consuming, and it has its shortcomings. For instance, their hardcover books are printed as case laminate, which means they do not have a dust jacket and the art is printed directly on the cover, giving the product an unpolished textbook-quality.

To produce a typical hardcover version that is indistinguishable from a traditional publisher's books and includes a dust jacket, you must enlist a third-party POD service to print the book and then link it to your Amazon page. Just like with KDP, you'll need to register for an account and submit the information, along with a new ISBN. There are a number of format-specific qualities to address, some of which may require extensive work by a graphic designer, such as:

- desired trim size
- formatting, including interior and exterior margins
- black and white or full color

- form of binding (clothbound or case laminate)

- type of cover laminate (gloss, matte, or textured)

- page count

- quantity of books to order

If the hardback and paperback dimensions will be the same, then the same formatted PDF can be used for the interior text. At the very least, the barcode for the back cover will need to be changed, and you'll need a new iteration of the cover for the dust jacket option. Since the dust jacket flaps customarily contain the book's description and the author's bio, this information will need to be shifted from the back cover and replaced with either blurbs about the book or favorable reviews by those who were given advanced reader copies.

Once these steps are completed, you'll need to claim your hardback on Amazon. Typically, Amazon can detect and "link up" your hardback for it to be sold directly on your book's page, alongside the other formats. This is admittedly a lot of work that likely will not reach more readers, but a hardcover format can be beneficial for contributing to a "professional" image and furthering your brand.

SUMMARY

✍ A new title is traditionally published as a hardcover to create prestige, but once initial sales goals are reached, the norm is to then release the paperback version at a lower price.

✍ For most independent authors, publishing a hardcover is often much more trouble than it's worth, and may not have value.

✍ Although KDP offers a hardcover POD service, their process can be cumbersome and time-consuming, and it has its shortcomings.

✍ Enlisting a third-party POD service to print the book and then link it to your Amazon page is required.

✍ There are a number of design issues that may require the extensive work of a graphic designer.

PART VI

LAUNCHING YOUR BOOK

CHAPTER 25
Generating Publicity

One of the biggest benefits of publishing a book is it can generate free publicity. Being a published author can position you as an expert and allow you to promote your brand in a variety of ways. For example, you may be asked to appear on TV, host a podcast, speak on a panel, or provide a quote for an article. Your book helps establish you as an authority in your field and your voice will be asked to be heard, especially by the press.

However, the press will probably not seek you out, especially as a first-time author. So, the onus is on you to make the media aware of not only your new credential, which now presents you as a new source for their reporting, but also the release of your book, which in and of itself can be newsworthy.

Similar to having to attract readers, members of the media will not automatically know the value of you and your book without being told. Hence, you proactively need to attract attention.

Generating publicity requires producing a press kit. Trying to promote yourself without one is like trying to drive across the country without gas. You may have an ambitious goal, but you're not getting anywhere.

A press kit, also called a media kit, is a pre-packaged collection of promotional materials including documents, files, videos, and other materials about a person, company, or organization made readily available to the media to generate publicity.

If you're not sure how to assemble one, there are plenty of templates available online that can guide you. In addition, many authors include their press kits on their website as both its own page and as a downloadable PDF. So you can view what a similar author provides in their kit to gain ideas for how to best create and shape yours.

A press release is essentially a short and original statement that details you and your book while providing information, contributing a quotation, creating interest, or making an announcement.

Essentially, the overall goal of a press kit is to make it as easy as possible for the media to produce a story. They won't have to do much work to research you because you're providing them with all this information upfront. Members of the media are generally expected to contribute content on a regular basis. Hence, the less time and work it takes for them to deliver their story—either about you, or with you as a part of it, the more likely they'll do it.

Your press kit should include:

- A high-resolution file of your professional headshot.

- Your biography that includes any relevant achievements, awards, and experience.

- Any prior media coverage, with links or PDFs.

- Complete contact information.

- Links to your professional social media accounts.

- A complete summary of your book.

- Your book description.

- A list of the book's product details: full title, page count, publication date, ISBN, publisher, price, available formats, and where it's available to purchase.

- A full-resolution file of your book's cover.

- Selected reviews of your book.

- A list of books that are similar or comparable to your own.

- A short excerpt of your book.

- Suggested questions for an interview.

You might need to include other content that may be relevant to your book, subject, or profession. But only include material that makes your kit more compelling, as many novice authors will fill their press kits with non-pertinent information in an effort to stand out. Then, instead of being selected for airtime or featured in an article, their press kits end up ignored and glossed over in favor of more succinct pitches.

Ultimately, a press kit is a quick and concise way to tell a potential media member everything they need to know about you and your book. The easier it is to obtain, process, and transform this information as needed, the more likely they will write the story.

A press release is essentially a short and original statement that details you and your book while providing information, contributing a quotation, creating interest, or making an announcement. It's an easy way for a publication to obtain information from you in exchange for (hopefully) promoting your book.

Your goal should be to craft an insightful, but concise, summary that would be both useful and interesting to a media outlet's audience and, if possible, topical to the current news cycle. It should be sent via email to specific individuals who ideally report on a subject that is most related to your field. Email it to publications of any size and geographic—local, regional, national, as broad as appropriate—in which you think there would be a fit.

Include a well-written, but concise, cover message and links to your information. Let the release itself go into detail about you and your book, while your email should be no more than two or three paragraphs, with as few sentences as possible. Entice the recipient to open the email by using a very short subject line, ideally posed as a question. Then, if you haven't heard back in a week, follow up with a phone call, asking for the person by name.

Sending out press releases may be a matter of chance, but a media outlet may very well keep it on file to use if you, your book, or its subject matter are ever in the news. But know that they receive countless releases every day.

To give yourself the best chance of garnering publicity, you may want to consider working with a PR firm. They oftentimes can guarantee some degree of press coverage, but their services will come at a price.

Publicity comes in many forms and can be short or long lived. It could be a series of television interviews, a string or newspaper articles, or a brief mention in a business journal. But it usually doesn't happen on its own. It's important to start the process well before your book's anticipated release date to build anticipation, curate your audience, and then maximize all potential when an opportunity presents itself.

Once your book picks up some media attention, it can be easier to get more. It can then be leveraged to build your business, brand, and more.

SUMMARY

- Being a published author can position you as an expert and allow you to promote your brand in a variety of ways.

- Media outlets are much more likely to choose published authors as experts to quote or interview.

- The press will probably not seek you out, especially as a first time author, so the onus is on you to make them aware of you and your book.

- A press kit, which is a collection of materials and information related to yourself and your book, is essential to secure publicity.

- A press release is a short, original statement that details you and your book, and is an easy way for a publication to obtain information from you in exchange for promoting your book.

- To give yourself the best chance of garnering publicity, you may want to consider working with a PR firm.

CHAPTER 26
Garnering Reviews

When your book is first available for purchase, the only way potential readers can judge its quality is through the information you provide in the description and preview pages. If it is appealing, it may interest them to read your book. But there's an even better way to land your initial readers, and it's based on trusting the word of others.

Most people read reviews every time they browse for a product or service, as they often are a major influence in their buying decision. If they recognize a brand they know, or are impressed by what they read, they're more likely to choose that brand.

In the same regard, using the five-star rating system, a potential reader will seek your book's overall score. A high one will catch their eye, while a low one will make them immediately scroll away.

Receiving high-star reviews upon a book's publication acts as the seal of approval to indicate to other potential readers that your book is worth their time. Earning positive reviews will help further establish your credibility, legitimize your book, and build brand recognition like few other things can.

To initiate the early review process, the standard in the publublising industry is to release Advanced

Reader Copies. ARCs are one strategy of a book launch in which free copies are given to a select group of people to read before its publication. The expectation (but *not* the requirement) is that they will write and post a public review of the book upon its release. In this arrangement, they read the book for free, and you get a review.

Amazon's algorithm identifies products that spur activity. The biggest signal is partly sales, but reviews (both good and bad) are what often prompts the algorithm the most.

You might wonder, why give a copy away for a review when you may receive one from an actual sale? Because, to receive what is called an "organic" review, you'll have to wait for someone to read the book in its entirety and then submit a review after. This could take quite some time and there's no guarantee they'll actually write a review, as most readers won't. And when it comes to your book's rankings, time is of the essence. To gain visibility, you cannot rely on reviews to appear organically.

ARC readers all know the implicit expectation of submitting a review and they almost always do it. And while you absolutely cannot explicitly ask for a five-star review, your ARC readers will typically leave a positive one. These initial, often favorable reviews are very important to earning a high ranking.

Amazon's algorithm identifies products that spur activity. The biggest signal is partly sales, but reviews (both good and bad) are what often prompt the algorithm the most. Once these indicators are "picked up" by the algorithm, your book will start to rank higher within its categories and may even be pushed as a recommended item to potential readers. This all creates more sales, reviews, and a higher ranking.

As a rule of thumb, a paperback should be delivered to a specific person whose review would hold a lot of weight, while sending a digital version is ultimately best if you're sending it out en masse.

ARCs can start this momentum. And they can be especially useful for a first-time author who has no prior reading audience to rely on. Thus, if you want to ensure your book gets noticed, then you need to distribute ARCs and directly ask the readers to submit a review when your book is officially published.

While advance audiobooks do exist, the norm is to distribute either paperbacks or eBooks. Since a paperback will need to be printed and shipped, it's the more expensive option. Sometimes, though, the extra cost could pay off, depending on who you're soliciting to review your book. For example, if you're planning to give all of your followers an ARC, then an eBook is the most economically sensible option since it can be done at no expense by simply emailing a watermarked PDF file to everyone who asked to read it.

If you're seeking a specific person to read the book, such as someone well-known in your field or an industry expert, then sending a copy to their office will be more impressive and could increase the likelihood that they'll read and review it. As a rule of thumb, a paperback should be delivered to a specific person whose review would hold a lot of weight, while a digital version is best for sending out en masse.

If you plan to send printed ARCs, you will not be able to order bulk copies through KDP until the book is actually live on Amazon. However, there are vendors who can do a short print run. If you choose to do this, it would be pertinent to imprint a watermark, such as a large banner across the front and back covers stating that these are advanced copies and not for resale. It's unlikely that anyone would try to sell their copy, but this is a low-effort measure that will further project your level of professionalism.

Before ordering all of your ARCs, it's best to first review a beta copy as a quality check. If there is an unexpected production error, it's much better to catch it at the expense of one book rather than an entire case.

To determine how many books to order, consider the number of people who have asked for an advanced copy, as well as the number of people you are hoping will review the book. To ensure you have enough, order a few extra copies to have on hand.

If you're hoping to have a specific person read your book (who may not have necessarily asked for it), send them a copy through a courier, such as FedEx. Since a FedEx package must be signed for, it guarantees that it will be received and hopefully opened. If so, the person is likely to skim the back cover and flip through the first few pages. Including a highly personalized note to thank them for their consideration to read the book may cause them to write a blurb or review.

Whether the ARCs are distributed physically, digitally, or both, you should always obtain your reader's email address. Once your book is live, you'll want to send an automated message to gently remind your early readers to submit a review. This can be easily accomplished by utilizing an email automation service such as Mailchimp.

Amazon encourages ARC reviews to jump start its ranking system and prompt sales. They are a great way to kick off the book's release, raise a book's visibility, and grow a readership base. However, the reviews need to be staggered; otherwise, Amazon might flag them as being paid for or otherwise ill-gotten and remove them entirely. To avoid this, you should contact people on different days and separate the email list into different groups of readers, such as by one's location and industry, or whether they're colleagues, friends, clients, or industry influencers. This way, the reviews won't be posted all at once and Amazon's algorithm won't perceive this as an unusual pattern.

When it comes to kicking off your book's publication, distributing advanced reader copies is a great tactic to generate reviews. Reviews generate traction for your book, which leads to higher visibility and legitimacy for your brand.

SUMMARY

- Most people read reviews every time they browse for a product or service, as they often are a major influence in their buying decision.

- ARCs (Advanced Reader Copies) are given free to a select group of readers before publication with the expectation of a positive review when the book is released.

- Earning positive reviews will help further establish your credibility, legitimize your book, and build brand recognition like few other things can.

- These early reviews help in gaining traction, which can raise your book's visibility and rank.

- Emailing eBook ARCs is best if you have a large group of early readers, while shipping paperback ARCs is best if you have a select group of potentially influential readers.

- Before placing your entire order, it's best to first review a beta copy to perform a quality check.

- To invite a specific person to read your book, send a print copy in a FedEx package to guarantee that they will at least open it.

- Once your book is live, send an automated message to gently remind your early readers to submit a review.

CHAPTER 27
Establishing an Online Presence

In order to successfully release your book, you must make a coordinated effort through a variety of avenues, particularly through establishing an online presence. A strategically planned book launch and ongoing promotion will raise awareness for the book. You can capitalize on the book release to garner interest in your brand and create other potential opportunities.

A book launch is essentially a series of coordinated marketing strategies organized around the book's publication. To maximize its potential, the planning needs to begin at the start of the writing process. Assembling a readership base prior to publication generates initial momentum and interest, which results in a wider potential audience. Ultimately, this will lead to more sales, reviews, and attention.

A single event is not sufficient to produce lasting visibility for your book and help build your brand. The process requires more than one marketing campaign with a promotional celebration on the official release date, or just sending copies to prospects and clients. Rather, a successful book launch has multiple components in motion simultaneously, which is why it's imperative to start the planning process early.

Developing an online presence is crucial for marketing, particularly for a relatively unknown first-time author. Most marketing for companies and products has moved into online spaces, so that's where you'll reach a large portion of your potential audience.

A fundamental technique for creating an online presence is blogging, which will help to continuously promote your book and further convey information about your brand. The easiest and quickest way to publicize your book is to repurpose a passage from it and post it as an article. Adding an appropriate heading and including the book's title, as well as its Amazon link, will generate interest in your book and send traffic to your site.

Your posted content—be it videos, pictures, text, links, or any other media—should be relevant to your book, brand, or profession in order to maintain your followers' interest, offer value to them, and retain a position in the platform's feed.

Any time spent on promotional endeavors is worth the effort, especially when it comes to social media. To focus attention on your book (and not you personally), create a separate account for each platform. Twitter and Facebook are particularly prominent platforms to engage your audience, so be sure to focus your energy there first. Then, determine which platform(s) your target audience uses, such as an industry-specific site, and develop a following within this specialized group.

Be sure to start and maintain an account on every major platform—LinkedIn, Twitter, Instagram, YouTube, Facebook, Pinterest, as well as TikTok—even if you have no intention of regularly posting on all of them. At the very least, you'll be able to claim the same username for each platform and prevent other accounts from popping up under your name.

Your username should be as close to your name as possible. If your name is unavailable, simply add "author" or another term related to your brand, profession, company, or the book to distinguish yourself. Generally, the domain name should be short, easy to remember, and consistent across all platforms. Therefore, always check the availability on each platform before setting a universal username.

Having identical usernames not only creates a homogeneous brand, but it also makes it easier for your followers on one platform to find you on another. Similarly, all accounts should use the same profile picture, which is ideally your author photo on the back of the book. By using the same one, potential followers and readers will better associate you with your brand. Most platforms offer a link to your bio, which can be used to direct followers to your book's Amazon page, thereby creating the opportunity to make a sale.

Presenting a brief summary of who you are, your brand's message, and your book's subject will provide visitors with a succinct message to readily determine if they want to connect with you and possibly buy your book.

Your accounts need a steady stream of content if you expect to gain followers and grow an audience. To build your platform presence, you need to stay active through two main strategies: engaging with followers and creating content.

Following accounts similar to yours can help generate traffic to your profile. A platform's algorithms will "favor" accounts with activity, such as those that like, share, and comment on other people's posts, and push those accounts to more users.

Consistently creating content increases your visibility on the platform, both for your followers and other site users. An interactive and engaging account "scores" higher with the platform's algorithm. Your posted content—be it videos, pictures, text, links, or any other media—should be relevant to your book, brand, or profession in order to maintain your followers' interest, offer value to them, and retain a position in the platform's feed.

It's essential to regularly post high-quality content that will engage your followers to comment or share, since a high interaction rate will raise your brand's visibility. However, while it's important to post frequently, sharing irrelevant or poor content could lessen your brand's luster, and the platform's algorithm could even flag your account as spam.

Engaging posts could include:

- ✍ Asking a question for your followers to answer in the comments.

- ✍ Encouraging participation in polls related to your book or industry.

- ✍ Directly asking your followers to "like" a post at the end of a video or an article.

- ✍ Running a book giveaway.

- ✍ Collaborating with other similar accounts to create joint content for two different audiences.

Regularly posting quality messages that invite further engagement from your followers will raise your account's visibility and grow your audience. Establishing an online presence to promote your book will likely convert some of your followers into book readers and business clients.

SUMMARY

- A properly conducted book launch, followed by ongoing promotion, will raise your brand's visibility while attracting interest and generating potential opportunities.

- A successful book launch has multiple components that work simultaneously, which is why it's imperative to start the planning process early.

- Establishing an online presence is crucial for developing your audience and building your brand.

- An online presence refers to: your website, your ranking in related search results, and your social media accounts.

- Use the same username, profile picture, and bio for each social media platform to help potential followers and readers associate you with your brand.

- Focus on one or two core social platforms that are industry-specific as well as major platforms, such as Facebook and Twitter. ·

- Engage with other accounts and post high-quality content on a routine basis to help grow your following.

- By consistently creating content, a platform's algorithm will score your account higher and increase the visibility of your posts for your various followers.

CHAPTER 28
Building a Website

To help promote their book, an astute author will have a dedicated website and make regular updates with blog posts and other related material. Technology-challenged authors can still compose a professional site by using a SaaS website building and hosting company, which allow users to use pre-built templates and drag-and-drop elements to create and modify their own web pages.

The site should showcase your brand, immediately draw the viewer's attention to the book, and be simple to navigate. The easiest way to craft a visually appealing site is to utilize the "less is more" approach and keep the content simple. That may include limiting the use of excessive illustrations, odd fonts, or overly vibrant colors. A common font, two-color palette, and a design that conveys your brand are simple, standard features to make the most of your site. The graphics should be of professional quality and uniform across all platforms.

Potential readers will visit your website because their interest is piqued and they are looking to learn more about you and your brand. Therefore, it's important to display crucial information upfront. For an author's website, this means your homepage should display an image of the book's front cover, a link to every format available for purchase, and a condensed sales pitch (the 3 W's: *what* the book is about, *what* readers will gain from it, and *why* you're qualified to write it). The easier it is to access and understand this information, the more likely it becomes for a potential reader to buy your book.

The more high-quality content you have on your site, the higher up your website will be displayed in related search results.

Information can be effortlessly accessed when the website itself is easy to navigate. In addition to a homepage, an author's website typically includes these pages: "Books," "About," and "Contact." The "Books" page offers a one-stop place to list, describe, and link your book and any others you might have published. The "About" page presents a more detailed biography than the one you wrote for the back of your book. Your "Contact" page should include all of your professional social media accounts but *not* list your email address (which could invite spam). Instead, you can set up a contact form for visitors to send messages through.

Having the ability for viewers to sign up for a newsletter or otherwise receive emails from you is an option. You can use SurveyMonkey, Gmail, or any other data-compiling service to build an email list. However, only add individuals who have asked to be included and only email them information worth sharing, such as promotional articles related to your book's release.

You may also want to consider setting up a specific page for blog posts. Regularly adding valuable content related to your book will increase traffic to your site, earn repeat visitors, and boost your search engine optimization, or your SEO.

SEO refers to how the algorithms for search engines like Google calculate what web content gets ranked in their results. The more high-quality content you have on your site, the higher up your website will be displayed in related search results. This means more visibility, which leads to traffic to your site, and potentially more book sales.

To make your website as easy to navigate as possible, the norm is to include both a navigation menu at the top of each webpage and directly on the home screen. This will clearly organize your website so that all site visitors can understand it, and especially where to click to buy your book online.

It also needs to be mobile-friendly, since those people who are constantly on-the-go are likely to browse on their phone or tablet rather than their computer. A site that is solely formatted for a desktop is going to be more difficult to understand and will send many potential site visitors away.

While these requirements may sound exasperating, implementing them is easy with a site-building service. Keep in mind that DIY platforms will offer generic templates. So, if someone is familiar with the general look of these drag-and-drop websites, they'll often be able to determine that your website was not professionally designed.

And that's not necessarily a *bad* thing. If your site is clean and functional, it will leave no room for criticism or a question of your professionalism. Nonetheless, if you do want to present an extra sense of legitimacy, you should consider hiring a professional website designer, whether that means contracting a freelancer or a design agency.

If you have a lower production budget or would like to work directly with someone, then a freelance website designer is probably your best option. An individual designer is typically less expensive than hiring an agency, and the process will usually be a bit more personal. However, they may take longer to complete the project and the quality isn't guaranteed.

As with anyone, you always want to assess their portfolios and client reviews before committing to any one designer. If a portfolio is not automatically available, make sure to request a sample.

A design agency is often more expensive than a freelancer. Regardless of the price, you may want to choose an agency if you're seeking an established, streamlined service, many of which offer a money-back guarantee of your satisfaction.

If you have a specific design in mind, follow the reverse-search method: find a site that best matches your vision, try to contact the site owner to ask who built it, and then reach out to the designer from there.

Whether you choose an individual or an agency, always ensure they make the site editable so that its content can be changed or updated as needed. If you decide to create a blog, you'll also want to make sure you can regularly upload content on that page or have a link to your blog clearly displayed on your website.

A website helps establish your credibility as an author, clearly display your information for prospective readers, and boost your online visibility online, so it's important to do this correctly or to have it done by the right professional.

SUMMARY

- ✍ An author's website should showcase your brand, immediately draw the viewer's attention to the book, and be simple to navigate.

- ✍ Your homepage should display an image of the book's front cover, a link to every format available for purchase, and a condensed sales pitch.

- ✍ Regularly adding valuable content related to your book will increase traffic to your site, earn repeat visitors, and boost your search engine optimization, or your SEO.

- ✍ The more high-quality content you have on your site, the higher up your website will be displayed in related search results.

- ✍ An author's website can be built by using a site-building service or by hiring a freelance professional or a web design agency.

CHAPTER 29
Creating a Newsletter

When visiting most author websites, you'll immediately notice a banner or pop-up ad inviting you to sign up for their electronic newsletter. This is one of the most common, effective, and easiest ways to grow your audience and overall reach. A newsletter is beneficial to both you and your subscribers. They'll receive valuable information, and you can further their interest in your book and brand.

The best way to attract subscribers is by offering a free article or chapter of your book that promotes your brand in exchange for their email address. If they recognize the value, they'll be much more likely to join. In addition, providing an excerpt of your book can help sell it.

Writing and circulating a regular newsletter does not necessarily take too much time and work. The key is to repurpose parts of your book into a newsletter the same way you would with a blog post. It's important for the content to be high-quality, conducive to your brand, and worth your subscriber's time. It can be an avenue to build relationships with your readers (whether they are business prospects, industry influencers, or members of the media) by providing useful information, in addition to promoting your book.

As you capitalize on your newsletter to build your brand through sharing parts of your book's content, present your subscribers, who may have yet to read your book, with the opportunity to buy it at a discount or, depending on your distribution plan, receive it for free. Offering a special rate or extending an invitation for them to contact you to receive a copy—be it in digital or print form—will be perceived as a benefit that can build trust and your reach.

Your subscribers should have the sense that your newsletter provides valuable insight that others may not be able to access. If you're including low-quality material, pitching conspicuous advertisements, or presenting poor branding, they're likely to eventually unsubscribe or direct your emails to their spam folder. But by dispensing beneficial information from your book, you distinguish yourself and your brand, and position yourself for untold opportunities.

SUMMARY

✍ A newsletter will help you build a list of potential readers.

✍ Attract subscribers by adding an option on your website's homepage for visitors to sign up in exchange for a free article or sample of your book.

✍ Repurpose material from your book into content for your newsletter.

✍ Subscribers should have the sense that your newsletter provides valuable insight that others may not be able to access.

CHAPTER 30
Utilizing Advertising

When your intent is to build your brand, book sales should not be your primary goal.. The royalties received are unlikely to be a directly profitable return on your investment into this endeavor. Rather, your book is a vessel that can create opportunities for you, and that is how it pays off.

You don't write a book to make money—you write it to start a conversation. You write it to boost a brand that you're passionate about and want to share with others. Then, if your readers find value in you and your business, your book indirectly earns you money. So, to reach your goals and get to this endpoint often requires advertising.

Advertising to boost book sales can lead to a better known brand and an increased market presence. However, the amount to be allocated depends on a number of factors, but ultimately is determined by how and why it's spent.

There are countless ways to tout a book, yet usually just one reason: to promote or sell a product to as many people as possible. That being said, it's unlikely that your book needs to reach hundreds of thousands of people, but just those within your brand's niche. And, although your distribution plan may be to give away your book for free, you most likely intend to sell it. If so, then advertising might be worth its expense.

Leveraging your book to build your brand will direct attention towards your business and your expertise and, in turn, some of your readers are bound to become paying clients.

If done correctly, advertising should increase book sales. It may attract a paying reader whom you might not have otherwise landed, which would increase readership, and conceivably rankings and business. The same reader may be inclined to write reviews, respond to and reshare your social media posts, and even recommend your book to other people.

Leveraging your book to build your brand will direct attention towards your business and your expertise and, in turn, some of your readers are bound to become paying clients. And since the service or product you offer is likely more expensive than the price of your book, you'll likely reap the financial benefits for years to come.

The most effective resources to employ for an ad campaign depend on your audience and your budget. Subreddits and Facebook groups related to your book or profession are usually an excellent option. Another avenue is sponsoring relevant content on a blog or digital media site. Although the price can vary widely based on the platform's audience size, notoriety, and level of sophistication.

There are unlimited advertising options available at every price point. You can advertise directly on Amazon, through industry publications, as a sponsorship, on the side of a bus, via cable television, in church bulletins, and even through targeted or cost-per-click campaigns on Google and Yahoo. The best place to advertise varies by brand and its target audience. However, since Amazon has a hold on the book market, it may be one of your easiest and most effective options.

Your advertising needs to be reflective of your brand's message and likely to reach your target audience. And while it isn't guaranteed to increase sales, it can help take your book to readers you may never have reached otherwise.

SUMMARY

✍ To reach your sales goals often requires the use of advertising.

✍ Leveraging your book to build your brand will direct attention towards your business, and some of your readers are bound to become paying clients.

✍ Advertising to boost book sales can lead to a better known brand and, in turn, an increased market presence.

✍ Your advertising needs to be reflective of your brand's message and likely to reach your target audience.

CHAPTER 31
Positioning Yourself as an Author

Becoming a published author positions you to widen your brand more than ever. Your book can be the catalyst to speaking engagements, career advancement opportunities, and invitations to contribute to other publications.

Having a book that details your expertise can make you a sought-after speaker. While the allure is your book, your presentation doesn't have to focus on it. Instead, your book can be the segway to discuss your business and your brand. At the same time, your remarks can offer a glimpse into how your audience would benefit from reading your book.

People are more likely to buy your book after hearing you speak, so these opportunities are too beneficial to overlook. However, if you're not comfortable speaking in front of groups, you can still capitalize on opportunities to buoy your brand and book without immediately making yourself the center of attention.

You can meet with small groups to start, where you may feel most comfortable and confident. Bookstores and libraries are often the best places to approach about presenting a talk, and many are open to hosting author events since it can boost their business. It certainly helps if your community already knows your name or is familiar with your brand, so begin with making presentations locally.

But don't limit yourself to only book-centric businesses. Colleges in the area could be in need of experts to speak to a class or student club. Similarly, you can explore local organizations that are relevant to your topic and would potentially be interested in having you as a speaker.

While the number of attendees at your speaking engagements may not equate to the number of books sold, each presentation will increase your exposure.

Social media can be utilized to arrange speaking engagements as well. You can identify events happening near you on Eventbrite or Facebook. Live streams and other virtual events are more common than ever, especially since the COVID-19 pandemic. They will often allow you to reach a wider audience and don't have barriers that would otherwise prevent people from attending, such as distance, travel restrictions, or health concerns. Since you don't need a venue or organization to host your speaking engagement, it's as simple as creating a live-streaming event on your social media platform and hosting it from your office.

Self-made virtual events allow you to direct the conversation and choose your approach, such as exploring the topic through an interview or a deep dive of the information, or discussing its relevance to your audience. You can cover any subject that represents you and the book, which can be tied to your brand.

The more speaking opportunities you land, the larger the audience you'll reach, and as you progress, you'll find that speaking about your expertise and your book gets easier with practice. While the number of attendees at your speaking engagements may not equate to the number of books sold, each presentation will increase your exposure.

As your exposure increases, you'll discover that your status as an author, and now a speaker as well, helps you stand out among your peers. These added credentials could draw the attention of executive recruiters or top-level industry leaders who may offer new opportunities for professional growth.

There could be several equally qualified candidates who may be in consideration for a job or opportunity that you may be seeking. Your competition could be just as highly educated and skilled as you, and in a pool of equally accomplished applicants, it could be impossible to stand out. Being a published author and respected speaker could move you to the top. A book brands your abilities and expertise, and could be the defining qualification in landing a job or being awarded a bid.

Whether you're looking to advance your career or promote your business, a book is immensely helpful for expressing your knowledge, advertising your abilities, and distinguishing yourself as the superior choice over competitors.

Authors who are successful business professionals have tremendous knowledge that can be transformed into content for guest columns or feature articles in a variety of magazines, newspapers, and journals. Print and online publications such as *Forbes, Inc., Entrepreneur, The Wall Street Journal,* and several other national periodicals frequently seek guest contributors to share their expertise and offer their opinions on a variety of subjects, especially prominent topics in a news cycle.

Some first-time authors go on to write more books. One method to determine if you have the content for another book is to review all of the topics discussed in your premier book. Is there a chapter, section, or even a sentence that you would want to expand on? If you can take a lesser-developed idea or concept within your first book and elaborate to make it into a complete outline, then you might have the material to write a second book.

There are business professionals who have built an entire career following the publication of their book. Consider Tim Ferriss. His first book, *The 4-Hour Workweek*, propelled the now renowned early-stage tech investor and entrepreneur to write five other best-selling books, produce his own podcast with over 100 million downloads, and much more ("About").

Your book can be the springboard to increase your brand's visibility and raise your business's profile. It can be the conduit for you to share your core message and open doors for you to present more of your unique knowledge in a number of other ways, be it through mass media, speaking engagements, an increased online presence, or by publishing new content through other avenues.

You can formulate ongoing messaging that continually tells your followers why you're the right person for them to trust. When you establish yourself as a published author, many doors that you had never even seen before are suddenly wide open. The opportunities are limitless.

SUMMARY

- Having a book that details your expertise can make you a sought-after speaker.

- Live streams and other virtual events will often allow you to reach a wider audience and don't have barriers to access that would otherwise prevent people from attending.

- A book brands your abilities and expertise, and could be the defining qualification in landing a job or being awarded a bid.

- Authors who are successful business professionals have tremendous knowledge that can be transformed into content for guest columns or feature articles in a variety of magazines, newspapers, and journals.

Why Enlist BrightRay Publishing?

Publishing a book is one of the best ways to build your brand and distinguish yourself as an expert in your field. A book is a streamlined way to tell your story, in your own words, to your prospects and clients, and to a potential worldwide audience as well. It can position you ahead of your competitors and allow you to establish what makes your brand special. Most people can list a variety of attributes that set them apart, but few can claim to be a published author.

Writing a book is hard. It requires detailed planning and the commitment to work at it for hours on end. It requires spending money on the right professional services to transform your manuscript into an actual book. And it will take further expertise to promote it so that people will want to read it.

If after understanding and accepting these challenges you're not deterred, and if you have the energy and time to commit to completing it, then you can do this. It's not impossible.

Yet, you may discover that although you indeed have the drive, desire, and resources, you lack the ability to complete your manuscript. As you use this book to guide your efforts, you may find your manuscript lacking. You might not be able to express yourself as best as you would like. You might have trouble organizing your outline, conducting research, or arranging interviews. Editing and proofreading may prove to be harder than you thought. Enlisting a qualified designer could be more difficult than you anticipated.

These challenges and many others could mount and you may decide to set the project aside, take a break, or even give up. Or, you could consider enlisting outside help. *Why not?*

This book explains the publishing process, but it took years to define the steps for ourselves. Remember, Scott didn't write and publish his book on his own. He needed Zoe to help him finish it. While he certainly had industry expertise and material that he wanted to share, he struggled to put it into a book. Zoe knew how to translate his ideas into engaging content and write in his voice, and they published his book together.

You may be like Scott and lack the writing skills and specialized publishing knowledge. Or maybe you simply don't have the time. It doesn't mean you can't publish a book.

It's not a well-kept secret that most business authors don't write their own books. They usually have a professional help them, which makes perfect sense. Because they're not writers, they delegate by hiring someone with a better skill set or working with a business that provides a service they need. But publishing their book requires more than just writing a manuscript. That's only the beginning.

Your book is an investment. You're allocating your resources with the intent of producing a worthwhile return.You could exhaust your time and money while attempting to write a book that never gets published. In the meantime, you could be telling others about your project, only to be embarrassed if it never comes to fruition. Ultimately, your brand will be worth more if you achieve your goal in writing a book.

We've shared the benefits of enlisting the expertise of a variety of professionals to help you produce a book. But at BrightRay Publishing, we offer services for the entire publishing process: *We get the book out of your head and onto the page.*

Our streamlined operation alleviates the stress and work of figuring out the publishing process on your own. Our team writes your manuscript with you—in your voice. We stick to a set timeline to conduct the composition, editing, formatting, and design. Then, we publish your book at a fraction of the time and cost that it would take for you to do it on your own. If you're looking for the quickest and most effective way to get your story out there and maximize its benefits, let us know.

To learn more about the services we provide, please visit: www.BrightRayPublishing.com

If you'd like to discuss your book's theme and goals, and have one of our team members detail our entire cover-to-cover process, call us at 407-287-5700, or send an email to BuildYourBrand@BrightRay.com.

Think of Us as Your Personal Writing Team:

No Typing Necessary!

GLOSSARY

Algorithm: The process by which a site or platform determines how and what results are displayed. This specifically refers to the algorithms that generate the recommended items on Amazon and the search results on Google.

Amazon Best Seller: A product offered on the e-commerce site that sells more than any other in its category. This banner is awarded based solely on sales and can be given under any category available.

Amazon Rank: The numerical position that indicates how close (or far) a product is to the best seller in any given category.

ARC: The abbreviation for Advanced Reader Copy, which is a preliminary draft of the manuscript distributed to beta readers, critics, and others with the intent of generating feedback, interest, or reviews prior to a book's official publication.

Beta Reader: Someone who reads an ARC to provide the author with feedback, critique, or an overall impression of the book, in preparation for its final revisions. They are generally not a professional within the writing or publishing industry and are ideally within the book's target demographic.

Book Launch: A set of planned promotional initiatives to market and advertise a book's publication. The strategies and the degree to which they are utilized depends on the variances and goals of the book.

Brand: The particular story, name, image, or other features that are crafted and controlled for a business or individual to distinguish it from others.

Categories: The e-commerce version of designated sections in a brick-and-mortar bookstore, it is used to classify books into groups by theme, topic, or subject in order to determine a book's rank in its distribution platform.

Copyeditor: Someone who reviews and revises a manuscript on a micro level, including fact-checking, grammar, and other fundamentals.

Editing: The process of rewriting and revising a manuscript until it is ready for publication.

Editor: Someone who reviews and revises a manuscript at any point in its development. They analyze the draft at a macro level and suggest changes to the structure, tone, flow, or other major elements.

First Draft: The initial completed version of a manuscript prior to any edits.

Format: The product version of a book, whether it be paperback, hardcover, eBook, or audiobook.

Freelancer: A professional or a skilled individual who offers their specific services for an hourly rate or a flat fee.

Google Rank: The order in which search results are displayed on a Google page. Results are determined by relevance, authority of the source, and other factors.

Independent Publishing: The system in which an author directly publishes their work through a print-on-demand (POD) or digital distribution platform. Unlike traditional publishing, the author is responsible for the cost of their book's production, is not paid an advance, earns significantly higher royalties, and maintains complete autonomy.

ISBN: An abbreviation for International Standard Book Number, this is a 13-digit numerical code used for booksellers, publishers, and others to identify a book.

KDP: An abbreviation for Kindle Direct Publishing, which is Amazon's self-publishing platform.

KDP Unlimited: A program available on Kindle Direct Publishing for independent authors who exclusively enroll their books to reap financial and promotional rewards from Amazon.

KENP: An abbreviation for Kindle Edition Normalized Pages, this is the calculated number of pages that Kindle Unlimited members read of an author's books.

Keywords: The relevant words and phrases tagged to a subject that determine the likelihood that the subject will appear in a search result.

Layout: The interior design of text and any illustrations within a book.

Manuscript: The complete draft of a book prior to publication.

Online Presence: The digital visibility of an individual or business that can be measured by their existence on social media, publications, associations, Google rankings, and so on.

Organic Review: An unprompted and honest review written by an unsolicited reader of the book.

Outsourcing: The hiring of a freelancer or agency to complete a task rather than doing it yourself.

POD: An abbreviation for Print-on-Demand, it enables books, generally in the paperback format, to be individually produced and shipped via distribution networks after being ordered.

Press Kit: A pre-packaged collection of promotional materials including documents, files, videos, and other materials about a person, company, or organization made readily available to the media to generate publicity.

Press Release: An official, original statement delivered to the media for the purpose of providing information, contributing a quotation, creating interest, or making an announcement for public distribution and promotion.

Production Budget: The financial plan that specifies the sum of funds that an independent author will allocate to publish and promote their book.

Proofreader: Someone who reviews a manuscript to detect and correct mistakes with grammar, typos, formatting, and graphics.

Rough Draft: Another term for the first version of a manuscript.

Royalties: The percentage of the revenue from book sales that an author is entitled to; royalties are often higher with independent than traditional publishing.

SEO: An abbreviation for Search Engine Optimization, it is the process of improving the quality and quantity of traffic to a website, and targets unpaid traffic rather than direct traffic or paid traffic.

Target Audience: The book's intended readership who are most likely to be interested in the author's brand.

<u>Traditional Publishing:</u> The system in which a publisher buys the right to publish a book by contracting with an author to print, distribute, and sell their book through booksellers and other retailers. The author receives an advance payment and is paid a percentage of the royalties from the book's sales.

<u>Typesetting:</u> Prior to digitalization, this was the process of physically arranging the text of a book to make it print-ready.

REFERENCES

"About Tim Ferriss." The Tim Ferriss Show, November 3, 2021. https://tim.blog/about/.

"The American Revolution." The American YAWP. Stanford University Press, May 22, 2013. https://www.americanyawp.com/text/05-the-american-revolution/.

"Buying Choices: How Do Authors Get Paid?" The Society of Authors. Accessed November 2021. https://www.societyofauthors.org/Where-We-Stand/buying-choices/How-do-authors-get-paid.

Blanchard, Ken and Spencer Johnson. The One Minute Manager. New York: William Morrow and Company, 1982.

Goldberg, Justine Tal. "200 Million Americans Want to Publish Books, But Can They?" Publishing Perspectives, May 26, 2011.

https://publishingperspectives.com/2011/05/200-million-americans-want-to-publish-books/.

Piersanti, Steve. "The 10 Awful Truths about Book Publishing." BK Magazine: Ask the Publisher, Berrett-Koehler Publishers, June 24, 2020. https://www.bkconnection.com/bkblog/steve-piersanti/the-10-awful-truths-about-book-publishing.

Murphy, Mark, "This is the Month When New Year's Resolutions Fail—Here's How to Save Them." Forbes, February 11, 2020. https://www.forbes.com/sites/markmurphy/2020/02/11/this-is-the-month-when-new-years-resolutions-fail-heres-how-to-save-them/?sh=5318f3e9272f.

Wood, Gordon S. and Theodore Hornberger. "Benjamin Franklin." Encyclopedia Britannica, April 13, 2021. https://www.britannica.com/biography/Benjamin-Franklin/Achievements-and-inventions.

Thank you for reading!

If you've found value from our book, we'd be grateful if you would consider writing a brief review on Amazon. As you've just read, reviews can help generate interest in our book and, in turn, attract more readers. We want to share this information with as many people as we can.

If you'd like to learn more about the services we provide, please visit our website below.

www.BrightRayPublishing.com

ACKNOWLEDGEMENTS

From Scott

Thank you Scott Johnson, my first mentor, for beating computer science in my head.

Thank you Steve Luther, my friend, lawyer, and wine sommelier, for your business strategy, covering my butt legally, and getting me to try Grüner Veltliner.

Thank you Jason Barnard, my Knowledge Panel Yoda, for formally training me in the ways of the Google Knowledge Graph.

From Zoe

Thank you to Camren Rodolpho, my partner and best friend, for cheering me on. I couldn't have done any of this without you. To say "you are my rock" is such a cliche, but it's true. I love you.

Thank you to Joni and Bruce Rose, my grandparents, for the many meals and many words of encouragement.

Thank you to Megan Rose, my aunt, for the honest advice and support.

Thank you to Bruce Rose Jr. and Mona Ossa, my parents.

In no particular order, thank you to all my friends who encouraged my progress throughout the years: Angela Paola, Priscilla Villegas, Mary Marshall, Iman Bijou Gebara, Dani Zini.

ABOUT THE AUTHORS

Scott Turman is an entrepreneur, IT expert, and author. Prior to founding BrightRay Publishing, he wrote code and cryptographic systems for NASA, the Department of Defense, Disney, and other Fortune 500s. He lives with his wife and son in Orlando, Florida.

Zoe Rose is the Chief Creative Officer and cofounder of BrightRay Publishing. She received a B.F.A. in English from Florida State University. Under a pen name, she has written and independently published multiple top-selling fiction titles. She lives with her partner and cat in Orlando, Florida.

NOTES

NOTES

Made in the USA
Las Vegas, NV
14 May 2024

89925337R00118